Ronda Rousey:

THE BIOGRAPHY

"F*CK THE NAYSAYERS"

D1535573

Proud to be published, promoted and printed independently. Available for sale at Barnes an Noble, Amazon, CreateSpace, Apple, Smashwords, and Kobo

Printed in the United States of America

TABLE OF CONTENTS

PART I: PROLOGUE

PART II: GROWING UP

PART III: ENTER THE CAGE!

PART IV: EPILOGUE

PART I: PROLOGUE

Note from the Author

Hi. Whether you've bought this book or you're just browsing the internet, I want to thank you for your curiosity. In a world where information is a dime a dozen, it really means a lot.

This book is unauthorized. That means Ronda Rousey and the UFC does not endorse it. The information contained herein is based on publically available documents, blogs, photos, documentaries, and interviews. I have portrayed Ronda in an accurate light to the best of my knowledge. The chapters go into deep, personal detail regarding Ronda's life, but this isn't the tabloids. I have no reason to skew Ronda's image into something twisted and nasty. Hell, she beats people to a pulp and gets paid for it. Pissing this person off would be hazardous to my health.

Thanks,

Matt Demers

matt.demers@hotmail.com

Ronda Rousey: At a Glance

As of 2013, Rousey trains under Gokor Chivichyan of Hayastan MMA Academy and Edmond Tarverdyan of Glendale Fighting Club. Her manager is Darn Harvey of Fight Tribe management. She is the 2008 Olympic bronze medalist and is considered the number one 135-pound fighter and the number one pound-for-pound female fighter in the world by all major publications and promotions including MMARising, MMAWeekly, Sherdog and the UFC. She is the largest female pay-per-view draw in history and one of only four women to have headlined a major fight card in all of televised fighting.

> "First they ignore you, then they ridicule you, then they fight you, and then you win."
> — Mahatma Gandhi

Fight Time

The co-main event at *UFC 157* has just finished. Ronda Jean Rousey waits backstage as UFC's site coordinator, Burt Watson, screams, "This is what we do, baby!" She walks with her entourage towards the stadium's entrance. This night is special — it is the first time women will compete in the Ultimate Fighting Championship and only the second time women have headlined a pay-per-view...ever.

She waits for her entrance song to start. Seconds feel like minutes. There is nothing left to do now but perform. The hours of drilling — strength and conditioning, boxing, jiu jitsu, footwork and wrestling — the sum of her six-day-a-week regimen at five separate gyms — are behind her now. The media nearly suffocated her with camera crews and interview demands in training camp. But during the intense eight weeks before the event, she never faltered. In fact, the pressure of winning fuelled her resolve, adding an edge to her intensity.

The overhead stadium lights go out and the arena is black except for spots of eerie glow from cellphones and smuggled-in cameras. The crowd roars. She feels the energy of 15,000 Californians course through her veins. They stomp their feet in unison, and it pounds in her heart like a war drum.

Spotlights beam and strobes flash. *Bad Reputation* by Joan Jett and the Blackhearts blares over the house speakers. Ronda Rousey is ready.

She makes her way towards the cage, surrounded by security and her cornermen. Ronda is swallowed by an event that is larger than the match itself. She heads towards the center of the stadium where history and fate await...

THEN

France, 1429

Joan of Arc appears before the Prince of France claiming she is a divine warrior of God. Despite a culture that expected women to be obedient, meek and ladylike, the 17-year-old takes up a sword to protect her country. She survives battle wounds to the neck and head from the enemy, but ultimately dies at the hands of her own people, burned at the stake for heresy at the age of 19.

West Africa, 1851.

Seh-Dong-Hong-Beh leads a regiment of fearless, all-female warriors called Amazons. They're known for their intense, physical training and limitless discipline. Armed with Winchester rifles, clubs and knives, Seh-Dong uses her tactical genius to lead 6,000 women in an attack against the fortress of Abeokuta. Though unsuccessful against the modern canons of the fort, she left her mark in the history books of Africa. Forever.

Stalingrad, Russia, 1945.

Klavdiya Kalugina, one of the youngest and best Soviet female snipers at age 17, fights in the Battle of Stalingrad against Nazi invaders during WWII. Seventeen thousand other women stand alongside her, manning anti-aircraft batteries, tanks, machine guns, and airplanes. Three earn Hero of the Soviet Union medals — Russia's equivalent to the Medal of Honor.

Joan of Arc depicted on a 1505 manuscript. Illustrator unknown. Joan of Arc is one of Rousey's favorite idols.

NOW

Vienna, Austria, 1984

Ann Maria Rousey DeMars, formerly known as Ann-Maria Burns, enters the World Judo Championships in the -56 kg class. She becomes the first American to win a world judo title. Her other wins include the US Senior Nationals, US Collegiate Nationals, US Open, Austrian Open, and the Canada Cup. She later earns a PhD in educational psychology and two master's degrees while raising three daughters on her own. She is Ronda Rousey's mother.

New York, USA, 2001

Laila Ali, daughter of Muhammad Ali, fights Jackie Frazier, daughter of Joe Frazier in the first ever pay-per-view headlined by women. Ali would go on to win. She retires with an unblemished record of 24-0.

California, 2013

Ronda Rousey fights for the UFC Bantamweight Championship against Liz Carmouche in the second ever pay-per-view headlined by a woman and the first ever female UFC fight. Since her mixed martial

arts career began in 2011, she has become the
largest female pay-per-view draw on the planet.

This is her story...

Ronda Rousey. Photo courtesy of PedroGaytan

A Brief History of the UFC

It is 1993. Michael Jordan retires to play minor league baseball, the World Trade Center is bombed, and Kurt Kobain has a year to live. The UFC is off to a great start with their first event to be held in Denver, Colorado and offered on pay-per-view. Unlike today's UFC, where fighters combine aspects of different disciplines, the UFC of 93' is a battle of style versus style to determine, once and for all, which martial art is superior. Can a kung fu master take on a karate expert? Can a boxer knockout a wrestler? The entire purpose of the UFC is not to create a new sport, but to finally put these age-old questions to rest.

Fights are held, as they will be twenty years later, in an octagonal cage consisting of 750 square feet of canvas space. Fighters make their way from backstage via a small entryway accompanied by police officers, security, and the fighter's entourage. Fighters have entrance music, but no fancy showmanship or pyrotechnics are permitted in an effort to distance the event from professional wrestling.

The Octagon has changed little since the UFC's debut. Shot of The Octagon from UFC 74. Clay Guida vs. Marcus Aurelio with referee Steve Mazzagatti.

Photo courtesy of Lee Brimelow.

The first event, *UFC 1: The Beginning,* is a no-holds-barred affair with the exclusion of eye gouging, and biting. Matches are bare-knuckle and combatants do not carry mouthguards, making them extremely vulnerable to serious injuries.

There are no weight divisions — men with as much as 100 pounds of weight difference between them are pitted against one another. Blows to the groin and the back of the head are legal and there is no time limit or judge — fighters go until someone falls. Since the UFC does not plan for future pay-per-views, champions are decided in a single night via a sudden death tournament, forcing fighters to compete in multiple matches over the course of a few hours.

The fights of *UFC 1* are fast and brutal. Wrestling beats Taekwondo, boxing pummels karate and kickboxing prevails against sumo. But one discipline rules them all — Brazilian jiu jitsu. Its practitioner — an unlikely hero in the face of US culture where worshipping brawny action stars like Sylvester Stallone and Arnold Schwarzenegger have warped how people look at true strength. That is why the nation is dumbfounded when Royce Gracie, the night's smallest competitor at 176 pounds, dominates everyone in his way. Using jiu jitsu, Gracie applies technical prowess to grapple and use joint manipulation to submit opponents on route to a $50 000 prize. Since jiu jitsu relies little on striking and slams, Gracie, and his opponents leave the Octagon relatively unscathed.

The original plans are to make the UFC a one-off event, but the tournament's success, earning 86,592 pay-per-view purchases, leads to follow-up shows. UFC's future is bright, with Royce Gracie as its first superstar.

Popularity soars. Each show brings more spectators and pay-per-view sales than the last. But then it happens:

U.S. Senator John McCain watches a UFC tape in disgust. He begins an anti-UFC movement, deeming it "human cockfighting." Since the legality of combat sports fall under the jurisdiction of state law, it is McCain's goal to convince as many states as possible to ban anything that resembles UFC fighting. He sends a letter to each state and uses his political muscle to pressure senators into banning the sport.

By the late 90's, the UFC is barred from 36 states including New York, home to the king of all fight venues: Madison Square Gardens. Pay-per-view purchases drop and SEG entertainment, UFC's parent company, goes bankrupt.

Enter Dana White: a thirty-something aerobics instructor and college dropout from Manchester, Connecticut. Dana is a super confident everyman — good with the ladies and popular with men. He tries his hands at amateur boxing and uses his charisma to break into the MMA industry, managing UFC champs Tito Ortiz and Chuck Liddel. When he learns that SEG is selling the UFC, he contacts childhood friends and Station Casino executives Frank and Lorenzo Fertitta to purchase the promotion. The Fertitta's consultants think they are nuts, reveals Lorenzo years later in an interview with *Fighters Only Magazine*.

> *"I had my attorneys tell me that I was crazy because I wasn't buying anything. I was paying $2 million and they were saying 'What are you getting? And I said 'What you don't understand is I'm getting the most valuable thing that I could possibly have, which is those three letters: UFC."[i]*

White and the Fertitta brothers found an umbrella company called Zuffa LLC and they purchase the promotion. With new investment capital, corporate sponsorship, and better advertising, the UFC makes a second run.

Dana White revamps the UFC brand. His goal — turn UFC into more a sport and less of a spectacle to distance itself from the "human cockfighting". Strict rules are implemented — the introduction of weight classes, the banning of fish-hooking, head stomps, spiking, small joint manipulation, head butting, and kicks to the head of a downed opponent.

Attendance and pay-per-view purchases go up, but the gains are offset by a huge operating cost, and by the mid-2000's, Zuffa is $34 US million in debt.

The Fertitta brothers sit down with White to break the news to him — they are going broke trying to keep the UFC afloat. White takes it hard; his dedication to the UFC had been borderline obsessive. In a last-ditch effort the three owners capitalize on the popularity of reality television and create *The Ultimate Fighter*, forking over $10 million to pay for the production costs themselves. The show features up-and-coming mixed martial arts fighters competing for a six-figure UFC contract. The show not only films them training, but sharing a large suburban home with their opponents. There is no TV, internet, or access to the outside world. A house full of combatants that know they are fighting each other guarantees good television drama, but would mainstream America accept an underground sport?

In January, 2005, *The Ultimate Fighter* launched in a time slot right after *WWE Raw.* The show is instantly successful and continues to soar as the season runs its course. The finale features Forrest

Griffin vs. Stephan Bonnar and proves to be one of the most intense, back-and-forth fights in the history of all combat sports. The fight cements the UFC into the consciousness of North American sports fans. It is here to stay…

Royce Gracie. Photo courtesy of: Peter Gordon

*Royce Gracie would remain
undefeated for seven years until
facing problems against fighters with
collegiate wrestling experience. As
of 2013, wrestling stands as the best
base for a successful career in mixed
martial arts.*

The Rise of Women's MMA

Japan is the cradle for female mixed martial arts fighters, albeit a minor one. Most Japanese male dominated promotions hold female fights, albeit rarely. These include DEEP, MARS, Gladiator, HEAT, Cage Force, K-1, Sengoku, Shooto, and Pancrase. Finally, in 2001, the first all-female fight promotion, Smackgirl, begins selling out venues. Other successful Japanese female organizations follow. These included Ladies Legend Pro Wrestling, ReMix (a predecessor to Smackgirl), U-Top Tournament, K-Grace, and AX.

The explosion of female fighters in the US would not come for another ten years. In 2005, the success of *The Ultimate Fighter* results in a mixed martial arts (MMA) explosion in North America. The fan base becomes so large that several smaller promotions are founded, piggybacking on the UFC's success. The smaller promotions are willing to venture beyond the fringe of mainstream media, featuring female fights that the UFC, and a larger audience, is not yet ready for.

The timing is good for women's MMA in the US — just as North American interest in MMA takes off, Japan's MMA industry flops. Female Japanese fighters must travel stateside for work. Their experience strengthens the female MMA talent pool in the west and helps legitimize women's MMA as a whole.

But to truly make it, women need their own *Ultimate Fighter*. Not necessarily a show, but a similar catalyst to catapult female fighters into the consciousness of mainstream media. That catalyst would come in the form of a young, beautiful kickboxer by the name of Gina Carano, who would later move on to star in *Haywire, Fast & Furious 6,* and the lead in an all-female version of *The Expendables.*

With short black hair and matching oil-daub eyes, Carano has the look of a Russian spy straight out of James Bond. But that isn't enough. To be a true pioneer, her deadliness must match her Hollywood good looks.

Photo courtesy of Michael Dunn

Gina Carano was born in Dallas County, Texas, in 1982 to Dana Joy and Glen Thomas Carano. Glen was a quarterback for the Dallas Cowboys between 1977 and 1983. Gina played basketball, volleyball, and softball in high school and college and earned a degree in psychology at the University of Nevada before pursuing martial arts.

Carano started kickboxing through her ex-boyfriend Kevin Ross, a respected Muay Thai pro.

She started out with Muay Thai to stay in shape, but took to it so well that she began competing, achieving a record of 12-1-1. She was offered larger paydays in MMA and accepted an offer to participate in the first-ever sanctioned female MMA bout in Nevada. Using her superior striking, she won and moved on to larger fights.

May 31, 2008, Gina Carano fought Kaitlin Young at *Elite XC: Heat*. It was the first women's MMA fight to broadcast over a major television network. It did not disappoint, with Carano winning by a highlight reel TKO in the second round.

Carano had a lot in common with Rousey — a great fighter, naturally athletic, strong-willed and holding an undeniable allure potent enough to make her a crossover star. Carano was more conservative in front of the camera than her protégé, but like Rousey, she was well spoken and dealt with the pressure of the spotlight with grace.

Carano's biggest fight to date came in August of 2009, where she was set to defend the Strikeforce Women's Championship against a much bigger, stronger opponent from Brazil, Cristiane "Cyborg" Santos. The event broke new ground for women's MMA, being the first major MMA card headlined by women and set record MMA ratings for the Showtime cable channel, drawing 856,000 viewers.

Cyborg broke Carano's undefeated record with a TKO in the first round to become Strikeforce's first women's champion — and Zuffa's first female champion. As of 2013, Carano hasn't fought since the loss, opting for Hollywood film roles instead of getting punched in the face. Who can blame her?

Cristiane "Cyborg" Santos, at the weigh-in before the Strikeforce: Carano vs. Cyborg event in 2009. Photo courtesy of Michael Dunn

Carano's following, although impressive, wasn't enough to change UFC president Dana White's mind about women in the UFC, but it got his attention. The press began to ask if women had a future in the UFC for which he responded with a punitive "no".

But at least the MMA community was now asking questions…

"It's showtime!"
—Ron Rousey

PART II: GROWING UP

The Early Years

Ronda Jean Rousey is born to Ann Maria Rousey DeMars and Ron Rousey in Riverside County, California on the first day of February, 1987. Riverside County is mostly desert — miles of rock and sand baked under the unrelenting West Coast sun. Californians often refer to Riverside as a "smog belt" because of wind patterns that blow pollution in from the Port of Los Angeles and Long Beach, giving the horizon a burnt copper look.

The first fight of Ronda`s life wasn't in the Octagon, but the hospital. Born asphyxiated by her own umbilical cord, her body is limp and blue. The doctors assume the baby is dead, but little Ronda Jean never taps. She regains consciousness and recovers, but not without consequence.

It takes less than four minutes without oxygen for irreversible brain damage to occur. Those that survive after that mark are left with physical and mental disabilities for the rest of their lives. In the case of Ronda, it is less a case of "if" and more a case of "how much" damage is done. The diagnosis becomes a waiting game.

Ron and Ann Maria hope for the best and they watch over Ronda closely, looking for signs of developmental delay. Being devout Catholics, Mr. And Mrs. Rousey pray the girl will live a happy, normal life. But Ronda is abnormally quiet. By 16 months, she still babbles like a baby half her age. When she finally learns a few words, they come out so garbled that no one understands her. This frustrates the toddler, throwing her into mini tantrums.

> *"I just remember being frustrated all the time, because I knew in my head what I wanted to say, but for some reason no one could ever understand me; my words came out as gibberish."[ii]*

Another symptom develops shortly after she learns to walk and it troubles Ann Maria even more: Ronda begins to step on her tiptoes, or what medical specialists refer to as *toe-walking*. Toe walking is common when a young one feels overly sensitive to texture; a classic indication that a child is autistic.

Doctors and family members assume the worst — her speech problems, the toe-walking and the oxygen deprivation she suffered at birth all point to autism. Ann Maria decides to make the diagnosis official and she brings Ronda to a specialist.

For doctors to test such a young child, they first look at secondary problems that might cause autistic-like symptoms – hearing problems, IQ and/or lead in the bloodstream. If these symptoms are clear, like in Ronda's case, specialists resort to clinical observation — studying the child as she plays and interacts with others. The doctors observe Ronda and it doesn't take long for them to decide. The doctor tells Ann Maria that without a shadow of doubt, Ronda is *not* autistic.

Nonetheless, the girl's struggle with words continues — Ann Maria tells Ronda that she can have anything she wants for her birthday. She asks for a "balgren". Her parents never heard of a balgren before and neither have any of their neighbors or friends. Mom and Dad set out, with all three kids in tow, to seek out the mysterious gift in every toy outlet in Riverside and L.A. County, but no one seems to have heard of a balgren.

Finally, they come across a big-box Toys R' Us and search up and down the aisles for anything that might catch Ronda's eye. She doesn't see anything.

Tired and disheartened, Ron grabs the manager and says, "I don't know what a balgren is, but you need to find it, because we're not leaving here until you do."[iii]

They narrow the search down — she doesn't want a video game or Barbie doll. She doesn't want a Lego set, toy car, or the board game *Operation.* She doesn't want candy, a remote controlled helicopter, or a Muppet Show play set. Then, as they pass by Wrestling Buddies, a popular rag doll that can be body slammed, punched, kicked, or elbowed, Ronda's eyes light up.

"Is this what you want?" The manager asks as he pulls one of the dolls off the top shelf. Ronda gets excited, hopping up and down. They are on the right track, but this isn't the one Ronda wants. She points at the Wrestling Buddy wearing yellow and red and sporting blonde hair on a balding head.

"Hulk Hogan! That's what she wanted," AnnMaria says. Aka balgen.

The Hogan doll gives Ronda her first grappling experience. She drags Hogan into the living room, slams him, throws him up in the air, and lets him drop. She lands flying elbows and pummels him with wobbly hammerfists. She even executes a very primitive version of the notorious armbar that would one day become her trademark. It doesn't take long for the effects of Ronda's armbar to wear the balding, blonde man down. She rips Hogan's arms clean off.

Ronda brings her mother the amputated wrestler and Ann Maria sews the arm back on. A few days later, her mom spots Hogan — a double amputee again. Ronda and Ann Maria continue the pattern of sew-rip-sew until Ann starts using dental floss to reattach the limbs. Voilà, Hogan's arms become indestructible and Ronda continues to wrestle away with Hogan until she outgrows him.

A year goes by, but her speech impediment doesn't improve. Her bigger sisters, Maria and Jennifer, begin to understand Ronda's garbled language. They become her translators for everything.

"What is it that you want?" her sister Maria asks.

"A bookie," Ronda responds.

"A bookie? Oh, a cookie! Ronda says she wants a cookie," and it's settled.

Her speech problems carry over to life at school. Children bully her and even the ones that don't, prefer to play with kids that can talk. Ronda feels alienated and becomes shy. She cries every morning and begs her parents not to make her go.

Whether the bullying has an effect on her athletic career can never be certain, but many top-level MMA fighters including Georges St. Pierre, Bas

Rutten, Forest Griffin, Wanderlei Silva, Kevin Randleman, and Cung Le were victims of bullying in their early life. Do these athletes use fighting to compensate for their past?

UFC welterweight champion and one of the pound-for-pound best MMA fighters on the planet Georges St. Pierre. St. Pierre took up martial arts to defend himself against bullies.

Photo courtesy of Ryan Mallard.

Ronda's parents realize that she needs something to boost her self-image. She needs something to call her own; something to excel at. With her dad ex-Army and Ann Maria a former athlete, getting Ronda involved in sports is inevitable. It doesn't take the Rousey family long to realize that Ronda's safe haven is sports.

Her father puts her on the Santa Monica swim team. He sees her advancing faster than other kids her age. Ron encourages his daughter any chance he gets. While some family members are distracted by Ronda's shortcomings, Ron is already making grandiose predictions for his youngest girl. And highly accurate ones at that:

"You'll see, Ronda is a sleeper. She's going to surprise a lot of people someday. Ronda is going to be in the Olympics."

Ron takes her to every practice. He wakes little Ronda up at 3am, the fresh smell of his aftershave tickling Ronda's nose. "It's showtime," Ron says to her; his hallmark phrase which just happens to be the same phrase Michael Buffer, MMA ring announcer, will use before her main event fights many years later.

Off Ron and Ronnie go into the still dark morning. Swim practice becomes a father-daughter routine and they grow closer.

It's possible that if Ronda continued swimming, with her nose to-the-grindstone mentality, she would have blown girls her age out of the water. Literally. Maybe she would have won some national titles and eventually made it to the US swim team. Perhaps she would have continued to improve and compete in the Olympics, her father watching her from the stands as she stands on the podium and receives a medal. But that would never happen. Things were about to change, a new course charted.

"Life turns on a dime."
— E. Guerrero

The Catalyst

The Rousey family moves from Riverside, California to Minot, North Dakota where Ann Maria Rousey, armed with two master's degrees and a PhD, accepts a teaching job. Ron retires from Rohr Aircraft Industries and the family adjusts to their new life.

It is a big change for everyone. While January temperatures often reached 70 degrees in Riverside County, in Minot, it's six degrees below zero. But snow is a novelty that the Rousey children are unaccustomed to and the hilly terrain in North Dakota is perfect for fast downhill sledding.

If the Rousey family knew what awaited them in those shadowy hills, they would never have trekked them.

While Mrs. Rousey works, Ron stays at home. He decides retirement is boring and takes a job at Devil's Lake as director of research and development at Sioux Manufacturing. The plant is located 120 miles east of Minot and soon it proves too much for him to make the daily trek. He decides to stay in Devil's Lake during the week and drive home on weekends. With Ronda's communication skills not improving, her speech therapist suggests Ronda stay with Dad, where one-on-one time will allow her to develop her language skills without her sisters there to translate.

Ron and "Ronnie" (as he liked to call her) grow closer. Ron buys her a Barbie car and she loves it, leaping into the front seat, and steering her way around the front yard. She makes her way down the driveway and onto the gravel road. The car doesn't take well to the rough surface and Ronda grows flustered. She jumps out and pushes it from behind. The car slips away and she falls face first into the gravel. She cries and Ron comes running.

He scoops Ronda up and whisks her inside. He brings her into the bathroom where she sees the marks on her face. That day Ronda received her first lesson on inner strength:

"Look how tough you are!" Ron assures her as she weeps. He tells her again and again. He tells her how cool she is. How she can handle anything. Ronda begins to believe it. She stops crying. Ron sees something special in his daughter, even if no one else does. The way she tries so, so hard to communicate. The way she gives everything she has when she swims. He sees her burning desire to achieve no matter the odds.

Ronda returns Ron's love in kind. She is protective of her dad. When he accidentally shaves his moustache off Ronda cries hysterically. She tells other kids with her garbled speech: *"My dad can beat up your dad."*

Ron instills appreciation of the outdoors into Ronda. They race around in his pick-up truck with their German shorthaired pointer. He teaches her how to shoot a gun and hunt quail. They go rock hunting, Ronda with a sand bucket in tow, searching the banks along the roadside for a good one.

It is this connection with her father that will make the coming years especially hard on Ronda.

She will take it harder than her sisters. Despite Ronda's struggle with speech and school, she is a happy child. One night in the North Dakota hills will change all that.

It's an ordinary weekend in the Peace Garden state. Ron has plans to take advantage of the fresh snowfall. Minot's terrain makes for great tobogganing, with the highest peak of elevation being "North Hill," some 1716 feet up. Dad and the girls grab their sled and head for high ground.

They find a hill worthy of their curiosity. The girls feel the need for speed, but Ron insists on testing the waters. He climbs the hill as his daughters wait impatiently at the bottom. They don't see what the big deal is. How can anyone get hurt surrounded by soft, fluffy white stuff?

He reaches the summit and jumps on the sled. Ronda and her sisters watch as he pushes the slope behind him to get started. He descends, and gathers speed quickly, but the hill seems relatively smooth for sledding. The sled is shooting like a bullet now, but Ron maintains.

It's over before the Rousey kids realize what happened. Ron's sled slams into a snow bank and his body is flung forward. His body lands awkwardly. The kids wait anxiously for him to get up but he doesn't. They rush over to him.

Ron is in terrible pain and unable to move. The snow bank he collided with is now partially uncovered revealing a log underneath. His injury is bad enough that he can't be helped, and a rescue chopper is called in. The emergency crew airlifts him to the hospital.

The nurses look him over and begin to cut away at his coat and pants. Ronda thinks they are hurting him and she picks a fight with one. They rush him off for examination while the Rousey family awaits the news. Hours later, a doctor walks through the double doors with the news.

And it isn't good – although he'll live through the accident, the collision broke his back. Rehab will strengthen it, but a long road of painful surgery and sleepless nights lie ahead. The medical bills will be massive and Ron will require bedside care until he regains his strength.

Ron is taken to the operating room. The first step in his treatment is surgery — utilizing "spinal instrumentation" — a steel rod or rods are permanently inserted into the area of damage to support the skeleton. The recovery is grueling, painful and the risk of infection is high. The surgery is completed without serious complications.

Now is the time for Ron to get his mobility back. He grinds through the post-surgery pain and the loss of dignity as he depends on nurses to bath and move him. Days go by and Ron takes refuge in the worst being over. Yet, the pain continues and his strength doesn't improve. He is floored by strong pain medication leaving him lethargic and able to sit up for only minutes at a time. He can't work. He can't provide for his family and doctors are baffled that his progress is stagnant.

The doctors reexamine him and discover something unrelated to the crash. Ron is diagnosed with Bernard-Souiler syndrome, a rare genetic bleeding disorder with an incidence rate of less than one in one million.[iv] The disease prevents Ron's body from forming blood clots. This causes bruising and excessive bleeding thereby reducing the body's natural healing abilities. There is no cure and although not fatal on its own, in the case of someone with severe injuries, the prognosis is poor:

Doctors take into account Ron's age, the condition of his back and the outcome of his surgeries. They find that not only is Bernard-Souiler syndrome preventing improvement, it is actually causing regression. Ron's back is literally crumbling in on itself despite the rod's support.

They tell him the outcome without sugar coating it — Ron Rousey will become a paraplegic within months and regress to a quadriplegic soon after. His lungs will lose the capacity to breathe on their own and he'll need a ventilator to live. Bernard-Souiler will eventually kill him. He is given two years and is discharged from the hospital with pain medication and a large hospital bill. Bills continue to mount and Ron is fully aware that he is a financial drain on his family. He sees the around-the-clock care that will be needed in the coming months. The thought of being bathed, fed and helped to the toilet is too much for a former soldier.

For Ron Rousey, the final straw is the idea of his children watching him fade away in a hospital bed with tubes protruding from every exposed area of his body. He makes peace with his decision.

***

It is now four years after the accident; Ron has lived twice as long as the doctor's predictions. Ronda, now an eight-year-old, comes home from school. A priest is standing in the living room and Ronda sees her mother in tears. It is the only time Ronda sees her mother cry.

"*My mom was just like: 'It's about your dad. He went to heaven,'*"[v] Ronda tells *UFC Primetime,* tears streaming as she relives it. She has retold the incident to the media again and again. "*People love to ask me all the time because...doesn't it make a great story?*" Ronda asks the *Primetime* interviewer sarcastically. The tears flow easily even after all these years. Ronda recalls vividly her reaction to her mom's news:

> "*I knew she was completely serious, and I just started crying. I tried to get up to go upstairs, and I couldn't feel my legs.*"[vi]

Ron had driven his car to a nearby pond; the same pond he spent hours with his daughters skipping rocks and breaking the ends off cattails. He hooked a hose to the truck's exhaust and looped it back into his vehicle and went to sleep.

Ron left a suicide note which will prove, like many of his predictions, to be a chilling prophecy. He promises that "Ronnie" is set to do great things.

That she is special. That she will end up on a podium somewhere, somehow.

In the same way her childbirth set the stage for Rousey compensating for her bullied childhood, her dad's death was another twist of fate that brought her a step closer to her potential. The overused motto, "Whatever doesn't kill you makes you stronger" fits here, but don't tell Ronda that. She may not be comfortable with the idea that her father was a martyr for her success.

The connection is undeniable nonetheless — Ronda's desire to swim crumbles with the passing of her father. Competitive swimming was something they did together, making every practice thereafter a reminder of his absence. Ronda takes a hiatus from sports, content, for the time-being, to watch her sisters and mother practice a Japanese martial arts known as "the gentle way" — judo.

Ron Rousey with baby Ronda and sister.
Photographer unknown.

"One of the things I've always believed is not to be defined by other people's expectations,"

— Ann Maria Rousey DeMars

The Judo Years

The Rouseys no longer feel comfortable in their North Dakota home. Artifacts still scatter the rooms —Dad's chair at the dinner table, his aftershave and razors in the medicine cabinet. The Rouseys needed to start fresh again. For that to happen, Ann Maria decides to move back to California.

Back in the West Coast, kids tease Ronda beyond her ability to cope. She still has a speech impediment and the North Dakotan accent does her no favors either. Her mom pulls Ronda from fifth grade to home school her instead. During that year, Ronda attends Mom's judo class and watches her teach.

Judo is a traditional mixed martial art started in Japan in 1882. It focuses on throws, takedowns, and submissions. Distinct from other martial arts, judo is based on using the opponent's energy against them, throwing them off-balance and bringing them to the ground. Elite judo incorporates striking, but in competition, including Olympic judo, striking is forbidden. Prominent UFC fighters with judo backgrounds include Hector Lombard, Yoshiro Akiyama and Dong Hyun Kim.

If Ronda knew what dark secrets American judo hid from the public, would she be so apt to excel in the sport? Secrets so vile, that the truth is swept under the carpet of the national judo scene out of fear it could be the end of the sport in America. If she saw through the suit and ties of the corrupted officials, would she still be willing to grind through two workouts daily, six days a week? Maybe. But in the years after her father's death, corrupt or not, judo becomes the cornerstone Ronda Rousey needs to reinvent herself.

Mom is pleased to see her daughter's curiosity in the gym with Ronda becoming interested in rolling on the mat and trying the odd throw, but Mom remains skeptical about subjecting another one of her daughters to the sport. Expectations would be high and comparisons with her sisters unavoidable. Ronda's tendency to grow frustrated was also a consideration; she is not the reserved girl strangers perceive her to be. No. At home, she is unafraid to express her fiery nature.

Ronda fights with her sisters often. It doesn't help matters that her older sisters tell Ronda that she is an alien — brought to earth as a baby, and placed on the Rousey doorstop. During one of their scuffles, Mom warns Ronda not to hit her sister. She is content on spitting in her sister's face instead. When Mom grounds her, Ronda argues:

> *"I shouldn't be grounded because you didn't tell me specifically not to spit in Maria's face."*[vii]

Despite initial reservations, Ronda's pleas to practice judo convince her mom she can handle it. Ann Maria hopes judo will improve her daughter's social skills and build her confidence.

And Mom is the perfect tutor to build Ronda's skills. Ann Maria holds the rank of Rokudan (6th

Degree Black Belt). She began her judo career at the age of 12 at an Illinois YMCA. Ann Maria's style emphasizes on ground game and submissions – a result of a knee injury sustained as a teen. Ann Maria would find out many years later that her ACL — the ligament responsible for stabilizing the knee cap — was completely severed.

With the technology unavailable to repair it at the time, Ann Maria has a difficult time with stability on the feet. Twenty years ago, torn ACLs meant a death sentence for elite competitors, but Ann Maria adapts. Instead of practicing throws and tosses that require stable legs, she works on submissions and pins to the ground. It is the only way she can win. DeMars tells *BleacherReport.com* years later:

"My only prayer to win was to get them to the ground — armbar them or choke them out. Ninety five percent or more of the judo I did was matwork,"[viii]

Ann Maria Rousey teaching judo. Photographer unknown.

Ann Maria trains to counterattack judo throws. She learns to hang on and submit her opponent by grabbing an arm or slipping behind her competitor to choke them out. This new style is highly successful — she wins her first major competition — the USJA Junior Nationals at age 16. Two years later, she moves to Tokyo, Japan as an exchange student and refines her game under a well-respected Sensei.

If the mat at the YMCA didn't slip and come apart so many years ago, Ann Maria would not have suffered the ACL tear. With a stable knee, she would not have focused on her ground game, or have passed down her unique style to Ronda. Part of that unique style incorporates Ronda's trademark submission hold. In the Rousey family, *everything happens for a reason* seems to be the unspoken aphorism of their lives.

And if a single move could embody that aphorism it would be the Rousey armbar, an official Kodokan judo submission hold that can cause permanent damage to tendons, muscle, and cartilage of the arm. Ronda completes the armbar by grabbing the wrist of the opponent while using her legs as leverage, keeping the body pinned while Ronda extends the arm. She pulls the arm across her chest with the intention of hyper extending the elbow, causing it to "pop" or dislocate if the opponent does not submit fast enough. It is not uncommon for seasoned judo practitioners to have their arm dislocated in competition, only to pop it back into place and continue to compete the same day. Just another day at the office.

Judo black belt applying a jūji-gatame (armbar) against her opponent.

Photo courtesy of Scarface999

In an interview with Middle Easy TV, Ronda describes in detail what applying an armbar feels like:

"...like tearing apart a turkey...When you are trying to get the turkey (bone) off and you can feel the cartilage, bones and tendons coming off...it really is that exact feeling."[ix]

Ronda has both elbows dislocated in competitions during judo. Repeated dislocations is enough to cut judo short, which is why her mother decides it is not enough to learn how to apply it, but defend it as well.

"Always be ready," her mom often warns her. While Ronda is watching *Dragonball Z* in the Rousey living room, her mom creeps up behind her and easily plants the armbar. "Always be ready," she reminds her daughter. Mom wakes Ronda one morning; by the time Ronda realizes she is being attacked it's too late — she taps to the armbar once again. "Always be ready," her mom repeats. This guerrilla approach to training continues until Ronda's defense is impregnable.

The armbar isn't the only thing Ronda excels at. She's a natural overall. Steamrolling through girls in her age group and the age groups above her, Ronda feels joy in winning. It is a refuge from her father's death and criticizing classmates. It's a safe haven for her and she dedicates to dedicate to the craft fully.

And the dedication shows — at one particular judo meet, Ronda's judo team is matched against a rival club. For an extra challenge, she competes in the boy's division. The rival club throws their best at her, but she takes them out with relative ease, one after another. The rival club's head trainer grows frustrated.

"A girl? Beating my best guys? Who does she think she is?"

The trainer exacts revenge. Under false pretenses he recommends Ronda compete against men in the brown and black belt division. Not content with odds, he customizes the rules to nullify Ronda's greatest weapon — he bans armbars.

Ronda wins regardless.

Even though she began judo relatively late, at age eight, only five years later she competes internationally at the Korean Open. Success doesn't come easy. Ann Maria pushes her harder than most parents would their children. She gut-checks Rousey often. Ronda recalls one incident:

> *"I remember my first injury very well. I was 11 years old and I broke my big toe doing judo. To an 11-year-old this is a very big deal, so I stopped fighting and started to cry. My mother then made me run laps around the mat for the rest of the night. I thought she was just being cruel at the time, but she told me sometimes you have to fight when you're injured. You need to know you're capable of that. "[x]*

In a separate statement, written on her judo blog she has this to say about her mother:

> *"My mom has the highest concentration of meanness you can fit into 5'2"*

Four years later, when Ronda is 15, she skips class for the first time and heads to the schoolyard. All that stands between her and freedom is a ten-foot fence. She scales it, but lands awkwardly and snaps her foot.

As punishment, her mom sends her on a road-trip to northern California that weekend. Ronda must compete in a judo tournament hosted by the club aforementioned rival club. She enters two divisions, with no coach, and fights in eight matches in front of a crowd that wants nothing more than to see her lose. When Rousey asks her mom why she would do something so harsh, she replies:

> *"You won't always have a coach, the crowd won't always like you, and you won't always be healthy when you fight. You need to know you can win anyway."[xi]*

Ronda never skips class again.

As tough as she was on her daughter, Ann Maria knows a balance between trainer and nurturer is important. By the time Ronda is 16, the youngster has reached the international elite ranks, by which Ronda's training is handed over to Jimmy Pedro Sr. In an interview at Akari judo Club in Richmond, Virginia, Ronda explains why her mom chooses not to oversee her training:

> *"She taught me all she could but never insisted on being my head coach. And I'm glad she did because I really needed a mom, someone I could cry and complain to when training was over. You have to hate your coach some days, that's their job, and I didn't want to hate my mother."[xii]*

Sixteen is also the year that Ronda finally receives a boost from Mother Nature. Up until now, Ronda is small for her age; her gi so large that it swallows her frame and makes her look younger, meek. For all her accomplishments, Ronda's scrawniness holds her back from being Olympic material, but then it comes: in less than 24 months

Ronda grows from 90-pounds to 120, then 140, double her weight from when she first began training. Ann Maria can no longer do matwork with her — Ronda rag-dolls her without mercy.

With Ronda's skill-set improving, the stakes become higher — an Olympic medal now a real possibility. Ronda begins training at The Hayastan Academy run by Gokor Chivichyan, an Armenian judo legend who trains upper-echelon mixed martial arts athletes. The academy is notorious around Hollywood for its hardcore training sessions. Unprepared youngsters, including local football talent, have been known to pay the monthly fee, attend once and never return.

The academy puts Ronda through the ringer. She trains almost exclusively with men, an approach to training that would spill over to her UFC days. The men constantly out-grapple, out-throw, and out-muscle her, pinning and submitting her at will. Ronda is frustrated not because she is losing, but losing to men who work half as hard. Crying becomes a daily ritual and it brings solace from everyone. Everyone except Manny Gamburyan, a judo, and karate black belt who will go on to fight in the UFC.

Sweep after sweep, he takes Ronda to the mat only for her to get up and be swept again. She strains her ankles, her arm. When Manny grasps her gi and maneuvers, Ronda is whiplashed and slammed to the mat. While she cries, Manny warns: "Tighten your lower lip or I'll go harder." These gut-check sessions put Ronda in worst-case scenarios and instills the mental fortitude needed to train like a champion.

As a side-note, Manny's no mercy approach is a form of tough love. All elite gyms, of mixed martial arts and beyond, combine an element of cold focus with an undercurrent of love, of comradery. Years later, Manny shares his thoughts about Ronda's transition to mixed martial arts, and he doesn't shy away from his initial concerns, despite his callous approach with her:

> *"I never wanted to see her fight.*
> *She's a cute girl...I didn't want her to*
> *hurt her nose. But her toughness is at a*
> *different level. I know MMA people are*
> *saying it's not a girl's sport, but her*
> *mentality, that toughness, that's*
> *something everyone can appreciate"[xiii]*

Jim Rome:

Ronda, when the zombie apocalypse goes down, what is your survival strategy?"

Ronda:

"Fucking houseboats!"

Jim Rome Show interview, February 2013

Fitting In

Her success in competition does not translate well in high school, where tomboyish behavior is never encouraged. Ronda enters elite tournaments and returns with gold medals, but no one outside of the judo bubble seems to care.

Schoolmates pick on for her strong physique and her ears, which have begun to swell and harden, brought on by repeated injury. Grapplers and MMA fighters and fans know this as "cauliflower ear" for the way the ear "sprouts" from fluid buildup (The only way to prevent it is to drain the ear with a syringe, a painful and time-consuming process). One particular case of Ronda's cauliflower ear inflates to such an extent that it flips the ear inside out. Kids don't understand it and what kids don't understand, they often ridicule.

Ronda remembers the doctors treating her ears:

> *"...they cut open the whole side of my ear. And they put like a tube in it to drain it. And my mom was like, 'get in the car' afterwards. And I was like, 'all right,' and I got in, and she just drove me straight to San Diego to go train. 'You were supposed to train today.' And I'm like, 'mom, my head hurts, it's throbbing.' And she's like, 'just take a bunch of aspirin.' Aspirin is a blood thinner, and makes it bleed more, apparently. So like, my whole headband was just covered in blood ... And now*

my ear is just deformed for the rest of my life. "[xiv]

Despite the hallway glances and back-of-class whispering, Ronda isn't the word fumbling, home schooled girl of yesteryear. Now when she walks the halls and someone snickers, she squares off. Grappling with guys like Manny makes the largest of boys at Santa Monica High mincemeat in comparison. And it was *only* the boys that Ronda was interested in fighting.

This leads to standoffs on a regular basis. Most boys have too much pride to back down from a girl's aggression, leading to scuffles they soon regret. Each time follows a similar pattern — a quick stare-down ends with the culprit tossed on his back, staff bring Ronda to the office where she begins to cry, knowing that the principal would be calling her mother. Rinse and repeat.

All the while, Ronda's training continues to escalate in intensity. She trains under multiple instructors and in different gyms. Most weeks, commute time is 14 hours total. It isn't unheard of for Ronda to train judo, jog, and top it off with a 25-mile bike ride in a single afternoon.

It comes at a cost. Her training begins to eat away at other parts of her life, including school. When Ronda takes the plunge and begins training for the US judo Olympic team, she misses classes regularly. Her Spanish teacher disapproves. Ronda responds by dropping out.

But her tunnel vision pays off. She gathers enough momentum in the international scene and makes the Olympic team without a hitch. Ronda is now Athens bound, and at 17, the youngest judo competitor for that year. Her coaches decide that she is best suited for the 63kg class (139 pounds), requiring a strict diet, and once in Greece, a hard weight-cut.

Most athletes that must "make weight" use some form of "cutting". They achieve this by dieting weeks before hand, then dehydrating the body before the weigh-ins by reducing water intake and using a sauna to shed the final few pounds of water weight. After the weigh-in, athletes have up to 30 hours before the bout, and they use this time to rehydrate and eat to pack the weight back on. By fight time, contenders will tip the scales well over the weigh-in limit, sometimes as much as 30-pounds over (men usually cut much more than women because of the male body's ability to shed weight quicker).

Even though Ronda has the technical skills of a champion, it is uncertain she has the stability, being so young, to make the podium in Athens. The pressure she puts on herself — to achieve gold or nothing — stresses her out in the lead-up to the Games. *USA Today* doesn't help — they label her as US's best hope to achieve a judo medal — something extremely rare for American judokass to achieve. The US judo Team head coach and 1992 bronze medalist Jason Morris, is aware of the hype surrounding Ronda:

> "*Sometimes, it's unfair to lump all that on somebody,"* Morris says. *"But

let's face it, it's sports, and if you're good that's what's going to happen."[xv]

In her first match she is up against the late Claudia Heill, a well-respected Austrian athlete with several European Championship medals in her collection. Heill proves to be a very game opponent, beating Ronda handedly and going on to win silver. Ronda won her second match against Sarah Clark, only to have her dreams of an Olympic medal smashed with a loss via penalty against North Korea's OK Song Hong. She places 9th overall.

In Memoriam:

Claudia Heill (24 January 1982 – 31 March 2011)

Claudia Heill was Born in Vienna, Austria in 1982. In addition to her success at the 2004 Summer Olympics, Heill won silver medals at the European championship in 2001 and 2005 and bronze medals in 2002, 2003, and 2007.[xvi]

She placed fifth at the 2008 Summer Olympics and retired one year later. After retiring she coached junior judoka.

Her finest hour was undoubtedly her silver-medal winning performance at the Olympic Games in Athens in 2004.

"This had been her dream even as she began practicing her first judo attacks as a seven-year-old," said her longtime coach Hubert Rohrauer.

On March 31, 2011, Claudia fell from the sixth floor of her Vienna flat. It is unknown whether it was suicide or a freak accident. Her former teammate, Ludwig Paischer, was stunned by her tragic death, saying, "She was such a fun-loving, friendly person." Claudia Heill was 29-years-old.

"I fight emotionless."
—Ronda Rousey

Fighting Boys

In sixth grade, a boy at her school — much older and larger — instigates a fight with Ronda. Kids know him as the schoolyard bully and he decides Ronda is easy prey.

"Give me your lunch money," the bully demands. Even at such a young age, Ronda was vaguely aware that she was experiencing a cliché. He asks her again, but Ronda refuses. The bully grabs at her neck, but she counters, taking him out with a judo flip and he goes sprawling. He lands head first onto concrete and his skull cracks open. Bewildered and bleeding, the boy cries. School staff rushes him off to emergency and he receives staples. The police slap little Ronda with community service.

Not counting the prize money and small stipend she received for performing at the Olympics, most people assume Ronda Rousey began prizefighting in her MMA pro debut. Far from it. The first time Ronda fights for money isn't in Strikeforce, the UFC, or any promotion at all. Her first payday is at Palisades Park in Santa Monica. She just turned 15.

Like most high-school kids her age, she is bored and broke. To earn cash, Rousey and a friend hustle in the local park. They bet a group of guys that Ronda can beat them up. The loser pays $5. The boys confidently agree to the terms and they face off. In seconds, she has them tossed to the ground and submitted. They beg her to stop and they pay the bet. Ronda goes off to Starbucks for Frappuccinos. Just another sunny afternoon in Santa Monica for Ronda.

Even in those afternoons in the park many years ago, Ronda begins to notice she can draw crowds. Kids would gather and watch as she tosses and sweeps boys much larger than her. Everyone cheers. It isn't every day a 5'6" blonde is tossing guys twice her size and making them tap. And being the unlikely underdog, she is the fan favorite by default.

> "*It's happened to me a couple times* [referring to the crowds],*"* Rousey admits. *"Not in a sanctioned, legal way, but it was entertaining to everybody that saw it. I got applause afterward."xvii*

It happens again at the movies. She sits in a row next to her cousin and a friend for the premier of *Juno.* An obnoxious group of teens sit in the row behind them. They are loud and chatty the entire film, and it makes Ronda's blood boil. She decides to let it go, until a couple kicks from behind crank Ronda on the back of the head — an accident, no doubt, but still aggravating. Ronda festers until the film finishes. When the credits roll, Ronda spins around and grabs the culprits boot. She pulls it off and wheels it down the aisle.

"Learn some manners!" Ronda yells at the bootless girl. Her boyfriend doesn't take well to the feisty blonde's tone. Was he going to let this angry bitch talk like that to his girl? No, certainly not.

Boyfriend and girlfriend are not alone. They sit with six others, outnumbering Ronda and friends two to one. Ronda decides it isn't worth it, and her group makes toward the exit, but the noisy moviegoers have other ideas. They quickly flank around and cut Ronda off, blocking them off from the lobby.

"Get my girlfriend's boot!" The boyfriend roars at Ronda.

"I ain't doing fuck all!" Ronda shoots back. Things are about to get *rowdy.*

Ronda attempts to walk around, but the boy pushes her backward. The push, although a minor form of intimidation, changes the legal standpoint considerably. Usually, it is best for combat athletes to irk on the side of caution during confrontation, especially within the confines of California state law. The state deems elite martial artists a "lethal weapon", meaning, in the eyes of the court, there is no difference between assaults involving the use a knife or bat and assaults where the assailant is a judo black belt.

However, another state law makes that a moot point — blocking an exit, which includes refraining others from entering the lobby of a movie theater, is a form kidnapping. What does this mean for Ronda? Judo or not, she has free reign to kick ass.

Rousey grabs the boyfriend by his shirt with her left and pummels him with overhand rights. The boyfriend's group retaliates — one steps behind Ronda, grabs her neck and yanks her back, but Ronda's constant training makes her grip extremely powerful, essential for hanging onto an opponent's gi. She holds her grasp on the boyfriend and continues to throw wild haymakers at the flabbergasted kid.

A straight left drops him and he folds into a pile on the floor. Ronda judo flips the guy behind; he flips and lands on his back, the wind knocked out of him. The bootless girl goes for Ronda, but Ronda's cousin jumps in and shoves the girl, sending her sprawling into the seats.

Bystanders lucky enough to stick around applaud loudly. Someone phones the police and they arrive within minutes. When the girl walks down the aisle to retrieve her boot, someone clues her in about Ronda's martial arts background. The group press charges, but since one of them had blocked Ronda's escape, the case never makes it to court. Ronda looks back on the incident years later and laughs:

> *"The funny thing is my shoe came off because I was fighting in flip flops...so everyone was just losing shoes. I threw her shoe, I lost my shoe, everyone's looking for shoes ... It was one of those things that most girls go through."*[xviii]

A Useless Ronda Fact:

Believes in aliens and 9/11 conspiracies; not Bigfoot.

Running Away

It's 2005. Rousey is 18 and getting sick of the grind. Every part of her waking life is dictated by others — Mom, trainers, managers and the people expecting her to win. Mom bans her from hanging out with her two best friends — they're considered detrimental to Ronda's training. She cannot go to parties, or to high school dances and she has no time for a boyfriend. Weeks are filled with 14-hours' worth of sessions and weekends are spent traveling to tournaments. Even during downtime, Ronda is too exhausted to do much.

Her diet is just as Spartan. As Ronda grows out of her early teen weight class, she edges closer to malnourishment and making weight is always a looming issue (with tournaments taking place most weekends). She downs coffee to kill her appetite and stay alert. When Thanksgiving comes around, she watches her relatives eat turkey and mashed potatoes while she sucks on ice cube Popsicles.

Ronda succumbs to temptation one evening, gorging on a sandwich and potato chips. She immediately jumps on the treadmill, watches the calorie counter and doesn't dare stop until every bite is burned off. Coping strategies like these are common.

Her poor diet grows beyond the issue of just making weight. It becomes about body image and she falls into a two-year struggle with bulimia from age 17 to 19. Part of the problem comes from boy's teasing her in high school, pointing at her built arms, and calling her "Ms. Man". She cries in the mirror, hides under baggy clothes, and cuts her hair short.

The lack of eating affects her health. Starving throws her PH balance off, causing acid saturation in her mouth, leading to teeth erosion. She shows up at tournaments with vertigo and stomach pains. "Every bite brought heavy, heavy guilt,"[xix] Ronda says years later regarding her bulimia.

The issues bleed into her performance. She flies with her team to the 2005 World Cup in Leonding, Austria. The small well-to-do town is gorgeous, brimming with history and a clear view of the Alps. But there's no time to explore it. Ronda's there for one reason — gold.

But winning is the last thing on her mind. Ronda feels drained, with no desire to compete. All she wants is rest. Her coaches spot her poor morale, but tell her to suck it up and go for the win.

She tanks in the matches, achieving only fifth place, one of the worst performances in her career. None of judo's elite were there. Ronda hasn't just lost, but lost inferior competition.

Coach Pedro is furious and instructs Ronda to scout out the remaining matches. She disobeys and heads back to the hotel with her boyfriend. Pedro looks for her, eventually making his way to her room, where he catches them together.

Pedro is appalled. Ronda has a history of being thrown off the team, then invited back only to be thrown off again. This time Pedro insists it's for good — she is expelled from Pedro's tutelage and barred from his gym. Her mother offers no condolences.

But Pedro's rejection is a blessing in disguise. Without judo, Ronda is no longer anchored to her old life in anyway, and for the first time in ten years, she is not obligated to live by someone else's expectations.

It is a tense trip home from Austria. Ronda mulls over her future and gets in touch with a friend in Albany, New York. She spends time in her room deciding the best course of action. One night, she waits until the house is quiet and Mom is asleep. She packs her stuff and calls a cab for the airport. All without warning. Her mother finds a note the next day, but by then, Ronda is already in Albany.

Looking back, Ronda admits there were better ways to go about it:

> *"I didn't really have the courage to speak up for myself. Between my mom and my coaches, every single second of my day was planned out. I couldn't go to a single party, I couldn't go to a single dance. I couldn't have a boyfriend. I had a couple of friends that my mom thought were bad for me, and wouldn't let me hang out with. Two of my best friends, I was banned to hang out with. So I was just frustrated by my lack of control.*
>
> *And instead of being able to sit down and have a conversation with them and*

talk it out, I was scared to. I just put my
affairs in order, got myself a flight, and
*peaced out in the middle of the night."*ˣˣ

Ronda running away is one of the worst things to happen to Mom, second to Ron's death. While her mother worries sick in California, Ronda eats donut holes in Albany, mulling over a new beginning. She realizes the source of her frustrations — having her life scripted for her by coaches, Mom, and the people that expect her to win. She decides from then on that her goals and the way she achieves them will be her decision.

Moves to Chicago and Montreal follow. The autonomy builds her confidence and she pushes through her shyness. While living in Chicago, she musters up the courage to break up with her boyfriend of two years, forcing her to live completely alone, by the skin of her teeth. While in Montreal she survives off pita bread and cereal.

In a way, the move east is a spiritual experience — a young American's version of the pilgrimage to Mecca. She left the West Coast a girl and became a woman. But with that, like all things, the thrill of finding oneself fades and the honeymoon ends. Reborn, Ronda feels the empty hole in her life that had been there since her trip home from Austria; only now is it made clear. She writes in her blog:

"I think an active life eventually
becomes engrained in your brain. So
though these people wish for that kind
of life, if they ever start "livin' the vida

lazy," they must go nuts or get stir crazy after a while. "[xxi]

Rousey moves yet again — this time to Boston where her sister lives. She repairs the schism with Mom and contacts Pedro to beg for his tutelage again. He complies and she trains, watches her diet, and prepares for the looming obstacle next year where, instead of the Parthenon and statue of Theseus, there is the Temple of Heaven and the Tiananmen Square. It's Ronda's last chance to fulfill the predictions of her father's suicide note. She hunkers down, builds her conditioning to pre-Austria levels, sharpening her technique with renewed vigor and readying herself for one last shot at Olympic gold. Beijing draws near.

"When it comes down to it, I let them think what they want. If they care enough to bother with what I do, then I'm already better than them."

—Marilyn Monroe

The Comeback

Jimmy Pedro and Mom, although no longer dictating Ronda's life, still hold high expectations for her. Her comeback starts off with a bang — She takes silver at 2007's World judo Championships in the middleweight division and the bronze medal at the 2007 Pan American Games. She is now four years away from making her pro debut in MMA.

If this was film, the rest of this chapter would describe a clean break for the top; a comeback story where heart and mind blow past all obstacles. But this isn't Rocky. A burning desire is a flame struggling to stay alight, often smoldered by intense training and the pain of competition. Motivated or not, combat sports are never smooth sailing.

At the Germany Open, Rousey faces Edith Bosch from the Netherlands. Bosch is a foot taller and carries a larger frame, making it difficult for Rousey to power through her. The match is a stalemate until Bosch tries a risky move — a flying armbar. Bosch lands it and Rousey feels her elbow pop in several different places. Her arm has been dislocated.

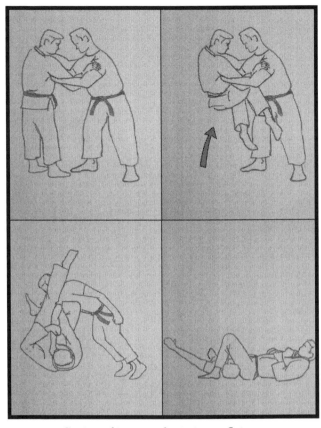

*Series of images depicting a flying
armbar submission. Artwork courtesy of
Kaan.uzun*

Unbeknownst to Bosch, the tournament forbids
flying armbars, disqualifying her from the match.
Rousey pops her arm back into place and walks off
the mat, her desire to continue in the tournament

gone with the excruciating pain. To make matters worse, it is also the 12th anniversary of her father's death. She sits on the sideline while a medic inspects her arm. He applies an icepack while Rousey mulls over what to do. She could drop out. The tournament isn't worth permanent damage. Live to fight another day? Sounds reasonable.

But one look at Pedro settles it. He stares at her from across the mat. His sullen glare screams, "Pull your ass together or else!"

Rousey continues bad arm and all. She wins bronze; another underwhelming performance. At the closing ceremony, officials hand her the trophy, but her injured arm is so weak that it falls from her grasp and shatters on the floor in front of a packed venue. Afterward, Pedro huddles the team together to congratulate them:

> *"You did a good job; you're all adults...go have fun tonight and don't get in trouble."*

Ronda isn't much for partying — she rarely drinks and never gets drunk, but thinks a little social time with her team might take her mind off Dad. The team showers, changes, and makes plans for the night's festivities. As they leave the venue, Pedro pulls Rousey aside and tells her she's done for the night. Her performance was disgraceful; he schedules a training session for her the following morning. Ronda can only take solace in the fact she can walk away anytime. But she doesn't.

Two months before Beijing, Pedro packs Rousey's schedule with tournaments. She competes in three over a span of four days. She injuries herself yet again in one of them, spraining her neck in the first round. She wins that match regardless, but doesn't dare show her discomfort with Pedro looming and the Olympics weeks away. Rousey walks on to the mat and waits nervously for her next opponent. If she injuries her neck further, she'll never pass the Olympics' stringent physical. Standing on the mat, Rousey scans the sidelines searching for her opponent, but she's nowhere in sight. After thirty minutes, Rousey bows in, bows out, and wins by default.

Beijing is next.

Ronda Fact:

Felt the first symptoms of arthritis at age 19.

Last Chance

Rousey makes a brash decision before flying out to Beijing and it shocks the judo community — Rousey will compete in Beijing at a higher weight class — 70kg (153lbs), a 7kg (15lbs) increase from her Athens effort. It is closer to her natural weight, and would require less cutting, but her ability to manhandle smaller opponents would be compromised. After initial reservations, Ann Maria agrees with her daughter's decision to move up:

> *"She's a model of strong now, instead of frail and anorexic."[xxii]*

Judo in the Olympics

Since its inception as an Olympic sport in 1964, judo has gone through many changes, expanding from four to seven weight classes. The scoring technique for the sport is complicated — points are given for successful throws, takedowns, and pins. Matches immediately end if a contender is awarded an *ippon*. This occurs if an opponent taps out, is thrown on their back with great velocity, or is thrown on their back or buttocks and is pinned for 25 seconds.[xxiii]

Rousey's trademark armbar is difficult to achieve under judo rules. The vast majority of her armbars are achieved while on the ground, but judo refs allow only a few seconds of ground grappling before halting the match and standing competitors up. To make matters worse, the time allowed on the ground is arbitrary, depending on the ref's or tournament's discretion. The small window of opportunity for Ronda to submit is ambiguous, forcing her to become extremely quick at applying it. When she later transitions to MMA, where refs only stand grounded opponents up after long stretches of inactivity, the time for Rousey to armbar will seem limitless.

Ronda Fact:

Biggest turn-off: guys she can beat up easily.

The Dark Side Of Judo in America

By now Ronda has racked up enough wins to earn a spot on the 2008 US Olympic Judo Team. This allows her to act freely (with little fear of being ostracized and prevented from joining the team), against a long buried evil within the US judo scene. She uses social media to uncover the truth:

Ronda begins a blog in 2007 called *Ronda Rousey (dot net!): Following the judo Life — from a blonder perspective*. She is witty, funny, and grammatically correct, especially for a high school dropout. Emails swarm Ronda's inbox from fans and haters alike. In one humorous post, she writes about a strange incident that occurred in her hotel room while traveling to one of her tournaments.

> *"Okay so yesterday the minibar guy came to the room to take all the stuff out of my fridge. But after he took everything out he turned around gave me four bottles of water, two mini bottles of wine and a coke zero. I thought that was pretty cool, but then like two hours later he came back with two Heinekens and said he feels like he met me 20 years ago. Now that was slightly weird but still nice I guess.*
>
> *Then this morning I wake up and he's standing there at the foot of my bed! I woke up going "What the F**K!" and the guy's so surprised that*

i screamed at him he gave me a Mars Bar and left.

I went back to sleep because I'm supremely jet lagged (I slept like 12 hours last night, not good) and when I woke up I wasn't sure if that actually happened or if I was just trippin' balls in my sleep.

But then I look at my bedside table and there's a mars bar, and I now had two extra water bottles in my room. So I'm double locking my door now."[xxiv]

Her blog is an open book, covering everything from her training and strict upbringing to her frustrations with the opposite sex. She writes quirky tidbits about herself – how she became a moderator of a Pokemon forum, her love of Santa Monica and things that annoy her.

The popularity of her blog is perfect for what lies ahead. By 2008, the US judo organization is rife with rumors involving the drugging and raping of young judoka — girls ranging from 12 to16 — going back as far as 1982. The accused, Fletcher Thorton, is still an active participant of the national judo scene, holding a high place within US judo organizations. United States Judo Incorporated chooses to do nothing about the complaints regardless of the multiple affidavits and witnesses. The organization assures active judokass that investigations are ongoing, but after 20 years, hold no one responsible.

The USGI insist that they did indeed investigate the first formal complaint, but no witnesses came forward to testify. Ann Maria, an active competitor in '82, recognizes that on paper the USGI may have officially investigated the case, but the organization failed to notify witnesses the investigation began. Without a testimony, the case collects dust.

Fast forward to 2005, — another formal complaint is submitted accusing Fletcher yet again. Most would assume that two complaints, submitted over two decades apart, would be a cause for concern.

Impatient with USGI, Ronda responds with vigilante justice. She uses the visibility of her blog and her popularity on judoforum.com to bring the scandal to light. Here is the original post in its entirety, where she shines light on the allegations against Fletcher Thorton.

> *My mom has a saying "Physical courage is the easy kind"*
>
> *So lets* (sic) *see how many people get mad at me this time.*
>
> *Everyone's in a rage over the refereeing from the trials. Well who's in charge of awarding ref ranks? Who is everyone sucking up to and making calls according to his preference?*
>
> *Non* (sic) *other than Fletcher - "the alleged" molester - Thornton*

Yeah I said it! I'll get real consequeses (sic) for putting that out there but I don't care.

Everyone was up in arms about Daniel Doyle, but USA judo didnt (sic) bat and eyelash at Fletcher Thornton's DOZENS of documented accusations of molesting young girls. One of our "A" referees even covered his eyes and refused to look at the police reports these girls filed.

And if you're a mod thinking of deleting this - yes this isn't small talk about "my first ukemi" but these issues need to be discussed. This is playing with the safety and careers of our athletes.

How is this man still allowed to be in the same VENUE of our athletes let alone protected by USAjudo and kept in an extremely influential position?

So yeah, this could be deleted pretty quick, so whatever I'll repost it on my OWN website, rondarousey.net, but I am personally outraged that this man is toying with the fates of our players, I'm sure my fellow athletes that got cheated out of their team slot - not to mention their family and friends would feel the same way. Or the young girls he "allegedly" molested, their families, and their friends !

No, I didn't get cheated - mostly because I never gave them a chance too - but I feel like I'm one of the few people in a good position to say something about it. I'm already on the team - try to stop me now!

If this man is not removed from office and banned for attending any and all USAjudo events by the time the olympics are over; I will NEVER renew my USJI membership or support anything to do with that organization again. And I would encourage my family, friends, and teammates to do the same.

Okay you can take you punches at me now, I'm braced and can take a hell of a hit.

***Please note I have said "allegedly" to prevent being libelous *** xxv

The message immediately goes viral within the judo community. Two weeks before the Olympic Games, Fletcher resigns. Her post was chancy, with a possible expulsion from Beijing. Ronda speaks in detail about risking her place on the US judo team in a subsequent post:

"Someone had to speak up against this pervert. I thought, if I'm the only one who has the balls to do anything about it, then I'll deal with the consequences. I got a hold of all the affidavits... Now, he's never going to be around judo or any young women ever. I felt obligated as a woman to do that." xxvi

Asked whether she fears being alienated from the judo community because of her accusations against Fletcher, Ronda responds:

> *"What are they going to do, throw me in judo jail?"xxvii*

Ronda's gamble pays off; the team keeps her place. With less than a month to go, her training reaches the pinnacle of tough — a three workout a day grind. She has mat burn so bad showering feels like washing in napalm.

Beijing arrives. Ronda flies with her teammates a few days ahead of schedule to acclimate to the time difference. There's plenty of time to reflect on judo during the 12-hour flight. What has changed since her Olympic debut in 2004? She is older, wiser, and more independent. Her arsenal has broadened, giving her more opportunities to win. She is stronger and healthier fighting in the 70kg class. But unlike Athens, can she now handle the pressure?

The plane touches down at Beijing Capital International airport. The team heads to the hotel and organizes their equipment. By this point, Ronda notices something has indeed changed. In 2004, there was tension — a fixation on gold or nothing. This time the pressure is gone. In fact, Ronda looks forward to it being over, to getting on with her life. Tuesday night, the day before she competes, Ronda sleeps like a baby.

Over breakfast, her teammate Sai says something to Ronda that she'll never forget:

"Dude, life is just going on as usual out here. The people in that building are stressing and battling it out and in their own little 'judo world' bubble, but life is just going on normally out here."[xxviii]

It mellows Ronda out even more. Her teammates and coaches can see the change in her, and comment on how relaxed she is, an unlikely attribute before big tournaments (and this was by far the biggest!).

The first match is against a girl from Turkmenistan, a judoka without a world ranking. This is usually a sign of inexperience, but Rousey is uncomfortable against unknowns, with no real way to gauge expectations.

As it turns out, her opponent is not ranked for good reason. Rousey immediately sweeps her for the pin. The match is over within seconds and Ronda is already miles ahead of her last Olympic attempt.

Rousey's next match is tricky. She is up against Katarzyna Pilocik from Poland, a competitor she's faced before. Rousey senses her opponent's nervousness. The Pole, afraid of being outgunned, drops low constantly, going for half-hearted maneuvers that stall the match. Rousey is forced to defend and comes close to receiving a penalty for her lack of offense. Rousey grows frustrated, but keeps it in check and looks for openings. With time running short, she makes her move. They roll, and Ronda grabs the girl's arm and yanks it. The girl's arm hyper-extends and she taps. Ronda celebrates her win, screaming to the crowd, *"I want a margarita!"*

She goes against Edith Bosch in the next bracket, the same Dutch powerhouse who dislocated Rousey's elbow using an illegal armbar at the Germany Open in 2004. Bosch's frame is massive — she looks a whole weight class larger than 70kg.

The fight starts competitive, with Rousey and Bosch coming close to earning points numerous times. Bosch's aggressive style is in full swing — she leaps in to get a solid grip on Ronda's gi, inadvertently punching Rousey in the face several times.

The match goes on for eight minutes. Bosch manhandles Rousey, but Rousey's cardio is miles ahead. Bosch's pace slows, and Rousey begins to dictate the match, instilling herself with confidence. Rousey lets her guard down briefly, just as Bosch manages one last burst of power. Bosh throws Ronda to the mat and the ref awards her a full point. Bosch advances. Rousey is no longer eligible for gold.

Rousey still has a chance for bronze, but she's already devastated. The relaxed, carefree girl from that morning is long gone; the thought of not medaling again unbearable. Ronda cries from the sidelines. She cries as she heads to the mat for her next match. She cries *during* the match and even as she scores points and advances on.

Her final match, now for the Olympic bronze medal, is against Annet Boehm from Germany — an opponent who defeated Rousey exactly one year ago. Preparing herself for a close match, Rousey is surprised to find that Boehm's morale is even lower than hers, making few attempts to score points. Rousey sweeps, earning points early on. Only a few minutes remain and Ronda switches to defensive play; her goal to run the clock down for the win. It is anti-climactic, but the clock reaches zero and the judges declare Rousey the winner. Rousey is now an Olympic bronze medalist and she becomes the first American woman to win an Olympic medal in judo. Ronda is ecstatic.

Ronda Rousey: Judoka extraordinaire
Photographer unknown.

The US Olympic committee throws an exclusive after-party for their US athletes. Most of the medal winners attend, including Michael Phelps, but he cuts himself off from the team. He has his own private room and bans athletes from entering. Ronda gives her thoughts:

> *"These NBA players over here are a bigger deal than this guy, and they're all hanging out with us. Hello, we're your teammates. We're not a bunch of groupies. Come hang out with us. Who the hell are you?"[xxix]*

She returns home and things change. MySpace messages fill her site from guys that ignored her in high school, now wanting to hang out. A publisher offers a book deal for an autobiography and assigns her sister, an ESPN editor, to help her write it (the author of this book is thankful that, as of 2013, the book is yet to see the light of day).

But her newfound popularity does not equate to overall success. The Olympic committee gives her $10,000 for placing third, which the IRS will tax later that year. The bronze medal bonus is enough to pay for half of her Honda Accord. Another run at the Olympic Games would mean four more years of training, travel and being broke. It would also mean frequent tournaments, which by now has put considerable stress on her body:

> *"Knee surgeries, separated AC joint, broken collarbone, broken more toes than I can count, broken foot, sprains in my knees and ankles. I've dislocated my*

> *elbow so many times that my ligaments*
> *are loose. I've broken my nose a couple*
> *of times; I have a deviated septum. My*
> *nose just squishes back, so I can get*
> *punched as much as I want and it's not*
> *going to deform. What can I say? It's a*
> *dangerous job."xxx*

Traveling to tournaments would also mean Ronda would have to pay for air travel and lodging up front. That would require a job to supplement her income. She takes a waitress gig at The Cork Bar and Grill on West Adams Blvd., Los Angeles and another at the pirate-themed Redwood downtown. One day, sitcom star Georges Wendt waltzed in and ordered rye.

> *"I served Norm from Cheers...I*
> *figured that was the Holy Grail of*
> *bartending."xxxi*

"Being broke is like a never ending cycle of wearing the same f'ing clothes and watching the same f'ing movies cause your broke ass can't afford cable."

— Ronda Rousey

PART III: ENTER THE CAGE

Road to MMA

After Beijing, Ronda decides to take time off in favor of a normal life. She enrolls in college, taking sociology and history of the Middle East. She hangs out with old friends and makes new ones. The new schedule is a breeze compared to her judo days. She gets up anytime she wants and workout when it suits her. For fun, she drives her Honda down Rose Avenue in Venice to hassle members of Penmar golf course. She honks at golfers during their backswing just to see them flip. How can hitting a little white ball be such a pressing issue?

Ronda loves the down time, but her cash flow does not sustain her. She is ambivalent when it comes to bank loans, preferring to live out of her Accord until she saves a rent deposit. If it wasn't for 24 Hour Fitness, she'd have no access to bathrooms or showers.

> *"There's nothing put in place for athletes. There's no scholarships, no job placement...I couldn't walk into anywhere and be like – Hey, I'm really good at throwing people down and breaking their arms; you wanna hire me?"xxxii*

The best the Olympic Committee could do — offer a part-time job at Home Depot. Luckily, friends tell her about the local Coast Guard base and it sparks her interest. Recruiters give her a tour and demonstrate emergency response drills. Impressed by her Olympic pedigree, they offer to negate the two-year waiting list just for her, allowing Ronda to

jump straight into boot camp almost immediately —
a once and a lifetime opportunity.

But there's a catch — a lengthy contract and
mandatory relocation every four years with no say
where. She googles "Coast Guard fatality rates" and
is astonished to find that the Guard suffers more
casualties than any other branch of the military,
including those with soldiers deployed to war zones.
It isn't worth it.

By this time, MMA is already part of her world.
While training for the Olympics, she lived with an
assortment of fighters, and trained with them. One
of those fighters was Rick Hawn, an upper-echelon
welterweight, fellow judo black belt and winner of
the *Bellator Season 6 Lightweight Tournament.*

She continues working out with Hawn and the
MMA guys, keeping her judo sharp without a
particular goal in mind besides keeping in shape.
One day each week, her judo coach spends time at
another gym, leaving Ronda and her teammates to
do as they please. On those days, the workouts are
less rigid, and MMA takes precedence. They crank
music and wear rash-guards instead of the gis.
Ronda instantly falls in love with MMA grappling
and dedicates herself to learning the nuances of the
sport. There's no denying it — judo is schoolwork;
MMA is recess.

Ronda doesn't seriously consider doing an MMA
fight, but her training partners are shocked when
they realize she can hold her own against seasoned
male MMA vets. Some encourage her to give MMA
a go, while others aren't so sure — she returns to

Jimmy Pedro and requests that he train her for an MMA fight, he is clear-cut with his response. She sums it up in an interview with *USA Today*:

> "He pretty much told me to go (bleep) myself."[xxxiii]

Her family agrees with Pedro. They tell her she is too pretty to get punched in the face. When Ronda asks Mom if she can move back home to train for a fight, her mother refuses. Ann Maria sees no financial future in women's MMA. At the time she was right — unless your name was Gina Carano there was none.

"Give me a year." Ronda pleads with her mom. Ann Maria reluctantly agrees not to criticize (but still forbids Ronda from living at home while training).

Acceptance (or at least tolerance) by her own flesh and blood is one thing, but acceptance in male-dominated sports, especially combat sports, has a long history of struggle. Ridicule outside of Ronda's judo network was common, but at least comradery on the mat brought solace. Now dismissal would be twofold — from outsiders and MMA athletes alike — including those she counts on to be training partners.

Women succeeding in prizefighting (where a decent payout and headlining spot are given) has been done, but only twice. Once, when boxers Laila Ali fought Jackie Frazier; another when MMA fighter Gina Carano fought Christiane "Cyborg" Santos. The Ali – Frazier fight isn't all that encouraging — Laila and Frazier were talented boxers no doubt, but it was their father's names that attributed to their success.

The Carano fight is different. Gina was the focal point. Her skill, undefeated record, and unquestionable beauty attracted a sellout crowd and record-breaking ratings. In other words, she was Ronda's spitting image.

But to properly prepare for professional fighting Rousey needs to train with elite MMA fighters at all costs. Her manager, Darren Harvey, brings Rousey to Edmond Tarverdyan of Glendale Fighting Club.

Glendale is simple as far as gyms go. There's a boxing ring, a large red and grey open mat, but no cage. There are a few treadmills, an elliptical trainer, stationary bike and a rack of free weights. Just the basics. To Ronda, it's not the equipment or a fancy hot tub that's important, but the athletes. They have talent, experience, and undefeated records. But would they want her there?

In an interview with *Sports Illustrated*, Tarverdyan is up front about his initial thoughts on Ronda's first visit to Glendale:

"I didn't think girls could fight."[xxxiv]

Tarverdyan doesn't take Ronda's ambitions seriously. He humors her, allowing Ronda to come in for morning sessions to train with the pros, but he refuses to coach her one-on-one. In fact, he turns a blind eye to everything she does in the gym.

Although Ronda tries to ignore the discrimination, it casts doubts in regards to whether there is a place for female fighters in MMA. One morning, Ronda sits on the edge of her bed and reflects on her past achievements. She is at a crossroad — since her speech impediment robbed her of communicating with others, many Tarverdyans have stood in the way. While in judo, naysayers envied her success and wanted her to fail. Schoolmates didn't understand the dedication, sculpted muscle, or tattered ears.

Instead of taking things personally, Ronda recognizes that their criticisms are merely a reflection of their own unhappiness. They surround themselves with reasons to not reach their own goals, justifying it by assuring themselves it is out of their control. This is a moment of clarity for Ronda. She knows what she wants to do and how to get it done.

> *"And it's taken me a long time, but I finally feel like I've realized what I want to accomplish next and made the decision to f**k all and go for it."*[xxxv]

There is no turning back. Ronda brings the same work ethic she instilled in judo and applies it to MMA. Three months into hard training at Glendale leaves an impression. She arrives earlier and leaves later than everyone else. She trains harder and is fearless in the face of men larger and more experienced. Finally, Tarverdyan gives her a chance and agrees to schedule her first amateur fight. This is Ronda's chance to prove her worth.

In the lead-up to the fight, Ronda begins working on the holes in her game — striking being one of them — and for which she enlists the services of

Main Event Sports Club. Unused to striking workouts — the constant mitt work, shadowboxing, and heavy bag sessions — leave her arms aching for days, something unaccustomed to after years of being in the gym.

Her coaches gauge her improvement and agree she's ready. Ronda and team decide her frame is best suited for featherweight, a weight class with a 145-pound limit (66kg), or nine pounds lighter than the weight she fought at the 2008 Olympics and only six pounds heavier than the weight she fought at in the 2004 Olympics — a weight that sparked malnutrition and bulimia.

With women's MMA still in its infancy, finding an opponent for Ronda proves difficult. Opponents that initially accept the bout bow out after googling Ronda and seeing stills of her in a gi, sending opponents (sometimes male) crashing to the mat. They see YouTube videos of her standing on the Olympic podium, bronze medal in hand. Would-be opponents want none of it.

Finally, Ronda's team snags a sucker. Rousey is to face Hayden "Diamond" Munoz on August 6, 2010 at *Combat Fight League: Ground Zero* in nearby Oxnard California. The event is held at West Coast Jiu Jitsu in front of a "whopping" 400 fans. The event screams "backwoods", with its poor lighting, wrinkled canvas, and a bearded referee looking like a cross between a Hell's Angels' biker and Gimli from *Lord of the Rings*.

Ronda's Olympic success gives her a high place on the card — the co-main event, an unheard of slot for two amateur fighters with records of 0 - 0.

She makes her way from backstage towards the Octagon. Tarverdyan and the rest of her entourage walk behind. Vaseline is applied, and her mouthguard inserted. Tarverdyan watches Ronda closely, and as he does, the last reservations he has about female fighters in his gym washes away. He sees her cold, focused stare, the unwavering intensity in her eyes, and he decides that win or lose tonight, Ronda Rousey will receive his full dedication. From then on, Tarverdyan sees Ronda the fighter, not Rhonda the girl.

The bell sounds and Ronda circles her opponent. Munoz throws a leg kick, but Ronda times it, charges forward, and sweeps. Munoz throws a few elbows and hammerfists from the bottom, but Ronda mounts, takes Munoz's arm and goes for the submission. She locks it in and Ronda wins by armbar submission only 23 seconds into the first round. The following morning, Tarverdyan reviews the match on YouTube and is astonished by the video's popularity — over 100,000 views. Training Ronda will be good for business.

Ronda takes two more amateur bouts, one of them a big leap in competition against Taylor "No Mercy" Stratford, an elite level striker with more experience, and half of her fights finished by submission or TKO. But Rousey's charge-and-grapple style proves too much for the 6 - 0 Stratford with Rousey picking up another armbar win in the first round. It will be Stratford's sole career loss (She retires in 2011, never turning pro).

Ronda's first pro fight is against a very game Ediene Gnomes, a Brazilian with a 6 – 1 record, and hailing from one of the most prestigious fight clubs in North America — American Top Team. There are pre-fight complications — days before, a pit-bull viciously attacks Ronda, taking a bite out of her foot. The bite is deep enough to reach bone and requires nine stitches, a good enough reason as any to cancel the bout. But with one glance at her bank account, Ronda has no choice but to fight injured. She wears socks during the weigh-ins and hides the cut from the medical team during the mandatory examination for fear they'd refuse clearance.

The fight goes as scheduled with Ronda realizing the inherent risks. The slightest trauma to the wound will cause massive blood loss and a TKO loss once the ref spots the damage. Luckily, her foot is never an issue; Rousey earns a flash finish by armbar in less than 30 seconds.

The Rousey armbar is more strategic than most people realize. She can apply it from multiple angles – the ground, standing, and behind her opponent's back. At this point in her career, with all her bouts won via the same submission, she knows her opponents expect it and will no doubt devote countless hours training to defend it.

But Ronda is already one-step ahead. She uses a cat-and-mouse strategy to lure opponents in. After a takedown, she purposely leaves holes in her ground-game, leading her opponents (specifically trained to spot these weaknesses) to attack Rousey's undefended arm, neck or leg. Ronda then counterattacks with an armbar from unexpected angles. The more her opponents work on their jiu-jitsu and wrestling to defend armbars, the more apt they are to recognize the "holes" and fall into her trap.

Despite her quick finishes, Ronda plans for her fights to go the distance (three to five rounds). She trains at Results Personal in Sherman Oaks, California to keep her conditioning topnotch. Her trainers have her lift heavy weight when she doesn't have a fight coming up, but in the weeks leading up, the exercises become more intense, and the weights lighter. Emphasis is placed on balance, conditioning, and explosiveness. One trainer in particular, Romanian elite wrestler Leo Frincu, is especially hard on her; his demeanor always cold and unwavering, Ronda tries to make Frincu laugh at her jokes, but to no avail:

"Pick up the pace!" Leo tells Ronda while she completes burpees.

"Do you mean the picante sauce?" She replies.

"Never tell that joke again," is Leo's only response.[xxxvi]

"I dare you to doubt me."
— Ronda Rousey

Enter Strikeforce

Ronda gets another armbar win three months after the Ediane Gomes fight, bringing her to 2-0 as a pro, with a 3-0 amateur record to back it up. Ronda's success in judo, and the fact that dedicated female fighters are hard to find, puts her career on fast track, placing her at the cusp of fighting in large promotions already.

And it's a good thing too. Six opponents have backed out the last three months, making the start of her pro career a testament to the early phase of women's professional fighting — shaky at best. Sure, bills were getting paid, with fight purses including free flight, meals, and transportation, but only the professionalism of an upper-tier company could assure her that long nights sleeping in the Honda Accord would never happen again.

In 2011, the largest MMA promotion housing female talent is Strikeforce. When UFC's parent company buys it, many assume Dana White, with his stance against women on the roster, will fire all female fighters. The first match in Strikeforce under the Zuffa banner reinforces this assumption, with spectators booing Julia Budd and Germaine de Randamie for all three rounds. Regardless, Ronda gets the call from Strikeforce scouts and she signs her contract that summer. It increases her visibility in the MMA community tenfold.

Joe Rogan, UFC play-by-play commentator, comedian, and host of Fear Factor, notices Ronda's potential. Being a taekwondo and jiu-jitsu black belt, he can spot legitimate contenders and he sees the potential in Ronda. After Ronda picks up her first two Strikeforce wins, both first round armbar submissions bringing her to 4 - 0, Rogan invites her on his podcast show —*The Joe Rogan Experience*. Eddie Bravo, jiu jitsu expert and coach, joins him as the co-host.

"Whoa, did you hear that?" Rogan says to Bravo after hearing a loud popping noise. [xxxvii]

"That's my neck...I'm like *Pop Rocks*, dude," Rousey responds with amusement.[xxxviii]

She cracks her back on command then lifts up her hands for the camera to see, makes a fist —all her knuckles crack loudly. It blows Rogan away. The popping hands are the result of gripping an opponent's gi in judo for many years. Grabbing ahold of someone only to have them rip the gi out of your grip puts wear on the joints and tendons of the fingers. They snap and pop each time Rousey closes or opens her fists. She tells of Rogan:

> "*I had to tape my nails down* [every match] *so they wouldn't get ripped off.*"[xxxix]

Ronda takes advantage of the podcast's exposure to call out the Strikeforce Bantamweight Champion Miesha Tate. It is unexpected, given that Tate is not in Ronda's weight division.

Does Rousey Deserve a Title Shot?

This is Ronda's chance to breakout from relative obscurity. She sees the bantamweight champ, Miesha "Cupcake" Tate, as her ideal opponent despite the bantamweight division being ten pounds lighter than featherweight.

But Tate is beautiful, and Ronda sees the allure of two attractive females going head-to-head. It's not only lucrative, but a potential game changer for women's MMA. The only issue that looms is not whether Rousey has the talent to fight for the belt, but whether she deserves a shot having never fought at bantamweight.

Fortunately for her, MMA often tows the line between spectacle and sport, choosing to put on big money fights that fans want to see, rather than fights that adhere to official rankings. Ronda knows this, and begins a steady stream of trash-talk against Tate in an effort to bully her way into contendership.

"You gotta make a splash so everybody knows you're in the water," Rousey responds when fans criticize the bad mouthing. Strikeforce sees Ronda's self-promotion gathering steam, making the likelihood of high ticket sales and record ratings a good one. Strikeforce makes the fight happen, scheduling it for March 3, 2012 and giving it a main event slot to boot. This is *exactly* what Ronda had in mind.

Reflecting on Ronda's pro career this far shows just how quickly things changed. It took her less than a year and a half to go from fighting in no-name promotions to fighting for the title in Strikeforce televised in prime time. If she wins, sponsorships and fight bonuses will pour over her, putting an end to her financial struggles and marking the beginning of a successful career. If she loses, the hype and her undefeated record will tarnish all that she's achieved.

Another question remains: can Ronda drop the weight? Bantamweights fight at 135lbs, even lighter than her weight at the 2004 Olympics. It was a struggle then, and will prove more challenging now that she is seven years older.

Weight Cutting: Ronda's Extreme Diet

Yet again, Ronda faces the daunting task of cutting weight while trying to preserve most of her strength and vitality in the process. She tries a risky, leading-edge diet — a hybrid between the Paleo Diet and Warrior Diet. Paleo (paleolithic) emphasizes eating foods that early, pre-agricultural humans eat — simple greens, nuts, lean protein, and fruit. Because dairy, wheat, and gluten are products of human interventions, Paleo dieticians consider them incompatible with human evolution, and therefore unhealthy.[xl]

The Warrior Diet applies to Ronda's portion control. She makes the switch from eating three to five small meals a day to eating just once, six days a week, with a full fast on Sunday. Her daily meal is a large one — she packs in all the vitamins and minerals her body needs into one portion (or so the theory goes).

For athletes training two to three times a day, conventional medicine has always recommended more meals, not less, to keep the body healthy. When an athlete's body doesn't have the fuel for intense workouts, it quickly cannibalizes itself to survive. This cannibalization process is called the "anabolic state", something a fighter do not want their body to be in when they train or step into the cage. It is common for elite fighters to be rushed away by ambulance the day before the fight when their body crashes from dehydration and malnutrition, an unavoidable problem of going anabolic to keep the weight off.

Experts oversee Ronda's radical one-a-day diet. Her nutritionists theorize that when the body is hungry, the brain sends a signal to search for food, flooding the nervous system with energy. When the body is full, it no longer needs to search, resulting in the body slowing down to preserve calories. Secondarily, the theory states, after food is consumed, energy is devoted to digesting it, leading to lethargy.

Preliminary studies regarding one-a-day diets have shown mixed results. Professor and lead researcher in Australia, Leonie Heilbronn, saw health improvements in mice — a reduction of cholesterol and insulin levels that indicate one-a-day diets can lower the risk of diabetes and heart disease.[xli] Other studies have shown the opposite is true.[xl] As of 2013, researchers have not conducted one-a-day diet studies on humans.

Ronda worries about psychological repercussions of restricting her diet again. She certainly hasn't forgot her struggles with eating, holding an event in 2013 called "Don't Throw Up, Throw Down Clinic" at Glendale Fighting Club to raise money for Didi Hirsch Mental Health Services, an organization that treats people with mental issues including those with eating disorders. In all, Rousey and company raised $11,800, with almost half coming from Ronda's own pocket.[xlii]

All-Star Athletes and their Strange Diets

Georges St. Pierre: UFC fighter

McDonald's Big Macs

Herschel Walker: *NFL Player*

Bread and salad once a day. Nothing else.

Michael Phelps: *Olympic Swimmer*

Everything – fried egg sandwiches, pizza, pasta, French toast

LeBron James: *NBA Star*

Trix (kid's cereal)

Usain Bolt: *Olympic Sprinter*

McDonald's Chicken Nuggets and Yams

Lyoto Machida: *UFC Fighter*

A glass of his own urine each morning (urine therapy)

Laffit Pincay Jr: *Horse jockey*

When cutting weight — one peanut daily. Nothing else.

Alen Bailey: *NFL Player*

Slow-roasted raccoon

"People care much more about hype than about actual results."

— Ronda Rousey

Tate vs. Rousey

Miesha "Cupcake" Tate is a FILA Grappling Champion, high school state wrestling champ and World Team Trials national winner at 158lbs. She amassed a 5-1 amateur MMA record before turning pro in 2007. She becomes the FCF Bantamweight champ before entering elite competition. After a tough unanimous loss to a top-5 opponent Sarah Kaufman, "Cupcake" rallies back to win five straight on-route to reach the Strikeforce Women's Bantamweight Tournament finale against Dutch kickboxer Marloes Coenen. In a back and forth stand-up war, Tate uses her grappling prowess to submit Coenen via arm-triangle choke in the fourth round.

The March 03, 2012 bout against Rousey will be Tate's first title defense. When asked what she thinks of her opponent, Tate doesn't hold back:

> *"I don't feel she's earned it, at 4-0 and having never fought at 135 [pounds]."*[xliii]

Ronda doesn't deny that other factors are at play beside her record. In a conference call with Tate, Ronda responds:

> *"I'm not dumb, you're not dumb. Really, if we push the 'hot chicks to fight each other for a title', it's going to get a lot of attention. That's why I'd rather fight Miesha for a title* [rather than the champ in her own weight class]... *Because she's good-looking and she's marketable."*[xliv]

Ronda is aware that she's taking a big risk. Title fights are always five rounds — two more than non-title fights. Without having gone past one minute in any of her fights, Ronda has zero experience fighting an MMA bout exhausted. Fighters with no experience going the distance often succumb to the dreaded "adrenaline dump", a biological phenomenon known as tachypsychia.

Tachypsychia or "Adrenaline Dump"

Tachypsychia occurs when adrenaline pumps through the body as a result of confrontation or physical exertion. Fighters often report that time seems to slow down, heart rate increases, and colors become more vivid. Although tachypsychia brings intense focus and increased strength, it is taxing on the body. Fighters that allow their emotions to run away with their adrenaline tend to burn out within seconds, zapping their energy and the desire to win and sometimes causing hallucinations. They are left unable to defend themselves and often take a large amount of punishment in a short time frame, leading to career-ending injuries and sometimes death. [xlv]

The fight goes down at the Strikeforce: Tate vs. Rousey card in Columbus, Ohio's Nationwide Arena. After an action packed co-main event, Rousey and Tate enter the cage and stand in their respective corners. Tate wears orange and blue, Rousey, black and white. The camera pans over Rousey. She looks toned, and healthy indicating her weight cut went well. She bounces in her corner, her glare fixed on the champion. Ring announcer Jimmy Lennon Jr. gives the introduction:

> *"Introducing first on my left, fighting out of the blue corner, standing at five feet six inches tall; she weighed in at 134 and one-half pounds, with a storied background in judo, she is undefeated in her MMA career with a record of four wins, no losses, all four wins coming by way of first round submission. Fighting out of Venice, California, please welcome the 2008 US Olympic bronze medalist in judo, the undefeated challenger: "Rowdy" Ronda Rousey"! xlvi*

The camera cuts to the raucous Columbus crowd then to the champion. Jimmy Lennon Jr. continues:

> *"And her opponent across the cage, fighting out of the red corner, standing at five feet six and one half inches, she weighed in the same as her opponent, 134, and one-half pounds, a long time wrestling stand out, her MMA record stands at twelve wins, two losses, with three knockouts and five submissions. Fighting out of Yakami, Washington, and tonight making the first defense of her title, ladies and gentleman please welcome the Strikeforce Women's Bantamweight of the world, introducing Miesha "Cupcake" Tate. xlvii*

The roar of the crowd is deafening. Before the bout can begin, the ref calls for Tate and Rousey to meet in the center of the Octagon. They coldly stare each other down as referee Mark Matheny announces the rules. It is customary for the fighters to touch gloves, but they refuse and return to their corner and await the bell. Both look ready to pounce.

Finally, the bell rings and the two take central position in the Octagon. Tate wastes no time swinging haymakers, but the wild shots give Rousey time to leap in and grapple. She takes Tate down. Rousey assumes top position with a tight headlock around the neck of Tate. 15 seconds have gone by.

Rousey transfers from side control to a standing position. Tate throws leg kicks from the ground but Rousey manages to avoid them and re-establishes top position. Rousey uses a knee to pin Tate's left arm, with her right elbow free to grind away on "Cupcakes" face.

Rousey grabs Tate's arm and cranks it, using her legs to hold the reigning champion down and pry her arm away. The armbar is now in place — Tate's elbow bends at an awkward angle and hyper-extends.

"It's already dislocated!" Stephen Quadros, play-by-play announcer, screams from cage side.

But Tate doesn't tap.

Rousey loses her grip and Tate escapes, making this the first time an opponent has freed themselves from her trademark move.

Tate rolls, gets to her feet and clutches Rousey. Rousey is bent over leaving Tate open to plant knees to Rousey's face one after another. Tate grapples Rousey to the floor and looks for a rear naked choke. Tate stands above Rousey on the ground. Tate throws a lunging punch and drops into the guard of Rousey. Rousey gets up and Tate grabs her from behind. They roll and lay on their side. Tate's legs hook around Rousey's waist, locking her in and allowing Tate to attempt submissions at will. It is only 60 seconds in, but already it's the longest fight of Rousey's career.

They scramble again and make it to their feet. They exchange strikes, but Rousey retreats to the center of the Octagon. Tate throws a kick, but it's blocked. Rousey steps in just as Tate throws a hard left, catching Rousey square on the nose. It is the hardest she's ever been hit and she retreats, but Tate makes the mistake of closing the distance. Rousey grabs Tate and executes a judo hip-toss, sending Tate to the canvas with Rousey landing on top of her. She holds Tate down with a side headlock. One minute and thirty seconds remains in round one.

Rousey gets the side mount and transitions to full mount. She rains down punches on until Tate is forced to roll to her side. Now Tate is on her stomach with Rousey continuing with ground and pound. The onslaught is only a means to an end — with Tate softened up, and turtled into defense mode, Rousey grabs Tate's arm, flips her over and gets the armbar again. There is no letting go this time. Tate's arm hyper extends even more than the first time. Rousey can hear her arm pop as it is wrenched back. Tate finally taps. Her arm is severely damaged.

The crowd roars. Ronda is the new Strikeforce Bantamweight Champion, but everyone is left wondering about Tate. Is her arm broken? Will this end her career? One thing is certain — people that questioned the mental toughness of female fighters were proven dead wrong. Days later, Tate updates fans on her arm:

> *"I basically tore everything. I tore the inner and outer sides of my ligaments attached to the muscles and bone. It actually pulled the bone off with the ligament and then I tore all the muscles around that. So it was pretty bad, but you know, to me it wasn't really that bad. I think that, I have the motto that as long as you get up one more time than you fall down then you are doing something right. So I'll be back stronger than ever."*[xlviii]

Tate would go on to prevail in her next fight against Julie Kedzie (ironically enough, she won by armbar), putting her right back into title contention. She would later be signed by the UFC, but would lose her debut against undefeated up and comer Cat Zingano.

Although he's still not sold on the idea that women have what it takes to fight in the world's premiere MMA organization, UFC president Dana White was watching the Tate – Rousey fight closely. With fans shelling out as much as $60 a month for UFC PPVs, he is under pressure to put on fights worthy of the cost.

And now the UFC needed new divisions more than ever. White signs a seven-year deal with FOX Broadcasting Company. FOX requires a large amount of UFC content for their network (non-cable) station and their new cable network called FOX: Fuel, Fox: Sports 1, and FOX: FX. That means, besides the 12 - 15 pay-per-view cards per year, the UFC must now put out 36 free-to-watch cards on FOX.

The addition of so many cards spreads UFC's superstars thin. UFC ratings depend on headlining recognizable names. If there aren't any, cards become watered down and viewers tune out. To counter this, White adds three new male weight divisions — featherweight, bantamweight and flyweight. But these new weight classes feature smaller men, and as with boxing, smaller fighters (usually) don't generate as much interest.

"If I get her (Kaufman) in a choke I'm gonna hold onto it until she's actually dead..."

— Ronda Rousey

Rousey vs. Kaufman

After the Miesha Tate fight, Ronda's stardom takes off. The media demands are unlike anything she has experienced. In an exclusive interview she says:

> *"I just started to really accept that there's no off-season anymore…It used to be that I had time to myself in between and then I would take off, and things would calm down and then pick up. But when there was really no break between those two fights* [Tate vs. Rousey and Rousey vs. Kaufman]*, I just realized that the media craze wasn't something that came in phases. It was just the way it was from now on."[xlix]*

Post-fight media demands include a guest appearance on the *Late Night with Conan O'Brien* and a visit to Time Square with Showtime's *All Access* to open NASDAQ with UFC champions Jon Jones and Frankie Edgar. She is now a mainstream star with the eyes of the world on her.

> *"I'm adjusting to everything being awesome all the time because I'm used to having eviction and food and dog food problems, cockroach and the gas is leaking problems and the water pressure is out problems, we have no hot water problems…"[l]*

But she continues to live modestly, sharing a cramped flat with her roommates in Venice,

California, only a few short blocks from Venice Beach. The beach itself is known for its boardwalk — a breeding ground for bohemians, bodybuilders, surfers, hippies, poets, and starving artists who pepper the area twenty-four-seven.

. Her place looks like a fraternity — overflowing ashtrays, overturned coke bottles, books, and empty shopping bags are scattered about carelessly. Junk litters the table so badly that there isn't room to set a plate. Notebooks are scattered in the rubble, and Ronda flips through one for a quick laugh. Black and blue ink scribbles the wrinkled pages — the notes are drunken text messages from the night before or an amusing thought too good not to be written down, like this one:

> "*I love scratching my scalp with ballpoint pens, I get to walk around all day with my head covered in scribbles and no one notices!.... not just that, i'm the only one who knows this notebook is covered in microscopic pieces of my scalp =D*"[li]

The front room has a wall-mounted flatscreen and its plug dangles in the air with no outlet to plug into. A couch sits below the front windows, unusable because another couch is overturned on top of it. Ronda doesn't mind the mess:

> "*I always hating being in those houses where you had to be perfect...the carpet had to be perfect and if you stained anything it was the end of the world...I don't feel like my carpet being*

*all one color really has anything to do
with my happiness"[lii]*

Before she can focus solely on her fight against
Kaufman, Ronda has an ESPN photo shoot to take
care of that afternoon. She is set to be featured in
ESPN's fourth annual *Body Issue*, where Ronda and
other elite athletes will pose completely naked
(albeit tastefully and without revealing any x-rated
body parts) for the magazine. She is just about to
drive to the studio with her best friend and
roommate, Wetzel Parker. She seems nervous,
cracking her knuckles and waiting impatiently by
the front door with her purse slung around her arm,
waiting for Wetzel to ready up. This is a great
accomplishment by the little girl in Ronda, the same
shy, bulimic youngster who wore sweatshirts and
pajama pants even when the thermostat pushed
passed 80-degrees Fahrenheit. Now there she is, off
to pose naked for the world. As Ronda and Wetzel
drive to the shoot, Wetzel says:

> *"I'm really proud of her... She's
> changed, as in she has a lot more
> clothes, but that's it...She's kept it really
> real...you saw the house. She's a real
> person."[liii]*

They pull in to the studio parking lot and a
photographer comes out to meet them. Ronda exits
the SUV and suddenly remembers she doesn't have
her Strikeforce belt — it still rests on the mantel in
Venice. Wetzel drives back to grab it.

Wrapped in a white robe, Ronda sits nervously
on a foldout chair waiting for the photographers to

adjust their cameras. A makeup artist looks her over and re-applies blush.

Ronda fears a crewmember will snap a cell phone picture of her naked and post it online. The makeup artist assures her there is nothing to worry about. They are professionals.

The ESPN shoot seems to go well, but Ronda will have a one-and-a-half-month wait before the magazine hits newsstands. On the day of the release, Ronda will come to realize ESPN has made a horrifying mistake.

In the meantime, a week later, another photo shoot demands her time, this one a mandatory promo for the Strikeforce: Rousey vs. Kaufman card. Rousey and Kaufman stand off camera until photographers instruct them to walk onto the set and stand face to face. For fighters, standing quietly for thirty minutes while staring down your upcoming opponent creates a lot of tension, but as the cameras pan around them, and they stare coldly in each other's eyes, Kaufman relaxes the mood:

"My left armpit smells, so I apologize for that,"[liv] Kaufman warns Rousey.

"They can't smell it on video, so it's all good,"[lv] Ronda assures her. They crack a smile.

With Ronda's fame building, Throwdown MMA apparel grants Ronda a sponsorship. The contract includes mandatory open workouts where she must wear Throwdown workout gear. With only days before the *Body Issue* release, Throwdown schedules her for a lobby appearance in Las Vegas' MGM Grand. A cage is set up — Ronda and her striking coach grab boxing gloves and pads from their duffel bag. Before they can begin, in walks the team from Cesar Gracie Jiu jitsu, a famous MMA gym that includes UFC stars Nick and Nate Diaz. Ronda is not the type to be star struck, having met Oprah without batting an eye, but in this case, Ronda turns from elite competitor to hardcore fan. She blushes, and grows excited and nervous to meet the Diaz brothers, like a prom girl just before the big night. She is invited to work out at their gym in Lodi, California, a small agricultural community 90 miles east of San Francisco. Ronda gladly accepts.

Lodi is not a safe place to walk alone at night. Neighborhoodscout.com lists Lodi's crime rate at 200 per square mile each year — five times the national average. Much of the crime spills over from nearby Stockton, hometown of the Diaz brothers. Stockton is even more dangerous, tenth most dangerous city in America in fact, a result of poverty, social assistance, and rampant child abuse. Although Nick and Nate's parents had never hit them, Stockton's abrasive environment molded their personalities into the bird-flipping, smack talking in-your-face heels fans know them for.

Anyone watching a Diaz interview might get the impression that the brothers have a chip on their shoulder, whether it's directed at an upcoming opponent or the intrusiveness of the media. Their interviews are often awkward, choppy, and angst-ridden. Nick would earn a shot at the welterweight championship against Georges St. Pierre in early 2013. It is his second chance to fight for the title after White pulls Nick from the fight more than a year prior for ditching media appearances and refusing to show at press conferences. When he finally does get his shot, he becomes frustrated at St. Pierre's grappling abilities, taking late swings at him after the bell. Ronda worries that the Diaz brothers will act just as disagreeable with her as they do everyone else.

She travels 320 miles north from Venice to Lodi. She walks through the glass doors of Cesar Gracie's gym where Nick and Nate are already warming up. *Will they like me?* Ronda thinks. *What if they think I suck? What if they're mean?* Unlike men in MMA, Ronda never feels like her reputation follows her to new gyms. While male fighters with similar notoriety are given respect by default, Ronda needs to re-prove herself at each new club.

Ronda stands outside the boxing ring while the younger Diaz, Nate, shadowboxes inside. A boxing coach spots the jewelry around Ronda's neck. His eyes grow wide and he points a finger at her.

> "*You got that gold chain around your neck? They'll* [street thugs] *come to you, snatch it and pull a gun on you...I'm not lying.*"[lvi]

Ronda changes into her rash guard and heads to the mat with Nick. Already, she is surprised to find his personality is nothing like the UFC portrays. He is quiet and shy. He doesn't say more than a few sentences that aren't fight related, but according to the people that know him, even a few words is a good sign. Ronda jokingly tells Throwdown in an interview after their session:

Back in Venice the following morning, Ronda waits impatiently for a stack of ESPN magazines to arrive by Fed Ex. It's been six weeks since the photo shoot and Ronda stands by the roadside waiting for the courier van, nervously anticipating ESPN's handiwork. Finally, they see a courier truck painted with Fed Ex's familiar white colors and blue and red logo. They grab the box from the smiling courier and rush to the porch. Ronda cracks the package open. They peer inside and gawk at the cover — Ronda's eyes widen, not believing what she is seeing. ESPN staff never told her she would make the front cover. Maybe they weren't sure at the time or maybe it was all part of the surprise, but there she was, plastered on the front of ESPN's fourth annual *Body Issue*, 2012.

She takes a copy to her mother's apartment. Opening the sliding glass door, she steps into the living room, magazine in hand. Ann Maria steps out from the bedroom, all eyes on the book.

"All right, mom; are you ready to have a heart attack?" Ronda asks and hands Mom the magazine.

Silence.

"Well, you could be *more* naked,"[lviii] Ann Maria finally says.

More silence.

"So, this is as naked as you're gonna get?"

Ronda assures Mom it is. She has no plans to give it up for *Playboy* anytime soon. In her own words, she doesn't like the idea of men seeing her "cash and prizes" for five measly bucks.

Back at home, Ronda boots her Macintosh, hops on the couch, and surfs YouTube in search for ESPN's "Behind the Scenes" video featuring herself on the set of the photo shoot. It is set to premiere that day. She finds the link is up ahead of schedule and she clicks "play". The ESPN logo flashes on the screen and a shot pans over Ronda being worked on in a makeup chair. Another shot features Ronda in a director's chair talking candidly about pre-shot jitters. Ronda watches herself on the screen and seems to enjoy ESPN's handiwork. But that doesn't last.

The video shows quick shots of her posing nude for the camera. At first its fine — clever angles ensure that Ronda's best bits are left to the viewer's imagination, but halfway through there's a hiccup, and it's noticeable enough for Ronda to catch it.

"That was boob!" She screams at her Mac. But maybe it's just her imagination. She hits the playback button and re-watches it again. Ronda gasps — ESPN unknowingly filmed a quick shot of Rousey's breasts and by now thousands have seen it. In fact, the top YouTube comment lists the exact second the slip occurs. Ronda is livid. She grabs her cell phone and dials her agent.

"Steve-o, we have an issue. The behind-the-scenes thing – you can see my boobs out at one point. They promised there wouldn't be anything on there. This is fucking bullshit! Tell them to take it down now!"[lix] Rousey hangs up and storms off.

An official launch party for *Body Issue* is scheduled in Los Angeles for that night. Ronda isn't in the mood for it.

She drives out to Los Angeles regardless and checks into the Westin Bonaventure where Annie Van Tornhout, showtime publicist, meets with Ronda one-on-one. Ronda is still clearly upset over the YouTube video — she stares at the floor and speaks in monotones. Tornhout does her best to comfort her:

"All the [ESPN] executives will be there [at the launch party to apologize],"[lx] the publicist tells her.

"It was up all day [the video]! Obviously they aren't checking their shit!"[lxi] Ronda exclaims.

"They [ESPN execs] told me that no one noticed it,"[lxii] the publicist assures her.

"The top ranked comment is: 'go to this part of the video, Ronda's totally naked!'"[lxiii] Ronda argues back. She is ready to break out in tears.

"I feel betrayed," she adds.

That night, a limo whisks Ronda away to Belasco Theatre. She looks stunning in black heels and an elegant, hip-hugging black and silver dress, but her mood remains sullen and the limo ride with her friends is filled with awkward silences.

But then her cell phone beeps. She grabs it from her purse and taps the screen. She breaks out into a smile, blushes, and claps.

"Oh, God! Every single time Dana White [sends a text to] my phone I freak out!"[lxiv]

"What does it say?"[lxv] Someone in her entourage asks.

"He says 'with all due respect you look amazing in ESPN. Congratulations.'"[lxvi] Her mood has instantly changed.

Within minutes she is walking the red carpet and flashing her charming smile. The paparazzi ask her if she's enjoying her 15 minutes of fame.

"15 minutes? That's it?"[lxvii] She responds playfully.

Barely two months ago, Ronda juggled three jobs, living off bulk food, and driving a car with a broken air conditioner. Now she's on the cusp of her first title defense, a title that her next opponent, Sarah Kaufman, believes she never earned.

> *"Knowing that I deserved that title fight...then Ronda comes on the scene...she made this big statements saying 'I want to fight Miesha Tate for the belt because I think people want to watch it because we're attractive...It's bullshit."[lxviii]*

Kaufman has a point. Ronda was 0-0 at Bantamweight, while Kaufman record was 15 – 1, and on a three fight win streak. There is no denying that Kaufman *was* and *is* the true number one contender.

"It's infuriating," Kaufman admits in an interview with *All Access*: Now is her chance to prove the title is rightfully hers.

Strikeforce officially schedules Rousey vs. Kaufman for August 18, 2012 at Valley View Casino in San Diego, California. The event will broadcast live on Showtime and Showtime Extreme.

Kaufman is a 27-year-old Canadian Jiu-Jitsu brown belt. She trains under one of MMA's most brilliant coaches — the infamous Greg Jackson. In terms of being a celebrity, Kaufman couldn't be less like Rousey. She's lived in the small town of Victoria, British Columbia her entire life. For her, there are no red carpet events, no flashing cameras, or ESPN cover shoots. No documentary crews follow her every move nor do interviewers drudge up events from her past. But without the burden of stardom, she enjoys a luxury that Rousey can no longer afford, like today, where she winds the week down with a Sunday nature hike. Her friend tags along.

"August fourteenth, I leave," Sarah tells her friend, referring to the upcoming bout.

"What day is your fight?" Her friend asks.

"The eighteenth."

Ask anyone in town and people that know Sarah say the same thing — "I know she's fighting soon, but I'm not sure when." Kaufman lacks the Rousey's attention-getting looks to draw,, but without the distractions that come with popularity, she is able to focus on what matters — training.

Sarah Kaufman at Strikeforce Challengers 3.
Photo courtesy of Kelly Bailey

Kaufman stood at the pinnacle of women's MMA in 2010 when, at 10-0 with 8 knockouts, she fought Takayo Hashi for the newly created Women's Strikeforce Championship. Fearing Kaufman's power, Hashi avoided engagements and Kaufman won by an easy unanimous decision. Despite the win, she was disappointed the fight went to the scorecards. She made it up in her first title defense, power-slamming Roxanne Modafferi in the third round for her ninth KO win. Even though Rousey is the champ, many consider Kaufman to be the world's true number one female fighter.

Back in California, it's now four weeks out from the fight; Ronda's team has rented her a corporate apartment in the nearby town of Oakwood, where she can be alone — away from her roommates and friends. She begins reducing her food intake even more than she already does, in an effort to make it close to the 135-pound limit. Ronda will shed the few remaining pounds by dehydrating herself in a sauna a few hours before weigh-ins.

She's finished the most intense part of her training, but the workouts continue and the reduced calorie intake make the last few sessions harder than they'd otherwise be. Fighters find this stage to be the toughest — the calorie restrictions fluctuating the body's hormonal balance, leaving fighters extremely emotional and susceptible to outbursts. On top of this, a women's ability to shed weight is much more difficult than a man's. Physicians warn that women making hard cuts can lead to permanent fertility issues and even outright sterility.

Ronda, like many elite fighters, feels the effects of calorie restriction and she begins to withdrawal into herself.

Bottles of supplements scatter the rented flat and laundry lies in high piles — keeping a supply of clean gear is a large job for anyone working out twice daily. It equates to four pairs of clothes daily, which, if you include shirts, pants, underwear and sports bras, adds up to 112 articles of clothing each week. That's a lot of folding.

Back at Glendale Fighting Club, Ronda steps into the ring and spars with Diana Prazak, WIBA Featherweight World Champion. Sparring is an important part of learning how to take a punch without panicking. Since Kaufman has some of the best KO power in all of women's MMA, Rousey needs to find a way to close the gap and use her judo without getting tagged.

Ronda's training camp wraps up. She heads to San Diego days ahead of time. She weighs in under the limit, after which she rehydrates herself and loads up on carbs to get her strength back, bumping her weight up to around the 140-pound mark.

August eighteenth arrives. 3,502 fill the Valley View Casino for $145,000 in ticket earnings. It's a far cry from UFC numbers, but the cable TV exposure is crucial for women's fighting nonetheless.

Kaufman and Rousey stand in their respective corners. Herb Dean is the bout's ref. Jimmy Lennon Junior announces the tale of the tape and shouts out his trademark "It's Showtime!" catchphrase. The same phrase Rousey's father whispered to Ronda every morning before swim practice.

The fight is scheduled for five, five-minute rounds. The fighters meet at the center of the Octagon where Dean recites basic MMA rules. "Touch gloves and make it official," Dean requests. Rousey and Kaufman comply, and return to their corner. The bell sounds.

Rousey rushes to the center of the Octagon and throws a flurry of punches to close the gap. She clinches up, and holds Kaufman against the cage. Rousey drags her to the ground and only 30 seconds into round one, Rousey goes for an armbar.

Kaufman rolls with the hold in an attempt to get away, but Rousey's grip is unbreakable. She gives a hard yank on Kaufman's arm and Kaufman's arm hyper-extends easily. Kaufman must either tap or suffer a broken ulna. Kaufman taps and Rousey retains her Strikeforce 135-pound title and picks up another first-round submission victory — her sixth in a row — only 54 seconds into round one.

Rousey allows herself to wind down after a win. She enjoys a night out after the fight, but hardly drinks. The real payoff is the next two weeks — she'll eat nothing but junk food, leaving her vegan aspirations temporarily in the dust for her favorite — chicken wings and pie a la mode. But the vacation isn't just a short experiment into hedonism; it's also a chance to recuperate from weeks of exhausting workouts and media obligations. She sleeps like the dead.

The morning after the fight, it dawns on her that her body is unexpectedly sore. In fact, she's more sore now than she was after sparring and grappling sessions with large, male fighters. To be this sore after a 54-second fight, where her opponent put up almost zero offense, is dumbfounding. Even the act of brushing her bangs makes her grit her teeth in pain.

The numbers come in for Strikeforce's ratings and it's good news — viewership was impressive with the broadcast peaking at 676,000 viewers for the main event. It is the highest rating for a Showtime card in 2012. Dana White looks on with approval. This is exactly what Ronda hoped for.

"I would beat the crap out of Kim Kardashian...Any girl who is like...famous or idolized because she made a sex video with some guy...and that's all that she's known for...Oh, I got my name from sucking dick. Now she's selling Sketchers to 13-year-olds."

— Ronda Rousey

Women in MMA: Fighting for Approval

Since its inception, the role of women in mixed martial arts has been a subject of debate. Some observers have treated women's competition as more spectacle than sport, while male fighters are quick to play patriarch — viewing women as something to be protected. In December 2004, lightweight fighter Takumi Yano refused to participate in a Pancrase event in protest of sharing the card with female fighters.

The UFC welterweight champ Georges St. Pierre, and one of the top three pound-for-pound fighters of all time, was non-committal about his support for a women's UFC division. In an exclusive interview, Georges supports their growing popularity, but admits, "Personally I have a hard time watching the girl's fights".

Ronda is quick to respond:

> *"It really upsets me that Georges St. Pierre is taking that stance. Because if we want the women to do well and to be accepted, we need to have the other champions within the sport supporting us and not merely tolerating us...If he has such a problem seeing me get hit, then fine. I'm going to be so annoying to him, that it won't bother him in the least bit to see me get punched in my pretty little lady face."[lxix]*

Spike TV, one of North American television's main supporters of MMA, and one of the first to take a chance with the UFC before it was mainstream, holds a poll on their *MMA Uncensored Live* talk show asking viewers:

"Are you comfortable watching women punch each other in the face?"

The poll, despite its poorly worded question, showed most fans don't mind, with 73% of Spike viewers choosing YES, they are comfortable with watching women get punched in the face.[lxx]

Outside of North America, acceptance varies. In 2013, Miesha Tate vs. Cat Zingano is scheduled for Stockholm, Sweden to determine Rousey's next opponent. However, after UFC execs find Swedes are disgusted by women's fighting in any form, they pull Tate and Zingano from the card to avoid protest.

Women's MMA is trudging through the same renaissance that male MMA fighting went through in 2007. After widespread banning, the sport adapted, educated the masses, and implemented new rules to differentiate modern MMA from the no-holds-barred slugfests from the nineties. Eventually, with time, money, and constant exposure, MMA made a breakthrough. There's little reason why women's MMA can't do the same.

"I'm the most dangerous unarmed woman in the world"
- Ronda Rousey

Enter UFC

January, 2011. The paparazzi from *TMZ* catch up with Dana White after he dines out at Mr. Chow's, White's favorite restaurant in Beverly Hills. *TMZ* crew ask:

"When are we going to see women in the UFC?"[lxxi]

Dana replies:

"Never...Never," he responds smirking, then enters the backseat of a black SUV, and his chauffeur closes the door behind him. The thought of seeing women cut, bloodied, mounted and hammer-fisted against the canvas repulses him. White rolls the window down and before his SUV heads back to Vegas White adds:

"It's bad enough when a guy is getting beaten up, but a woman?"[lxxii]

Soon after, fans accuse White of being sexist. He argues that he isn't; the true problem being the lack of good female competitors. Whether White is avoiding a hailstorm of criticism or telling the truth is debatable, but that doesn't take away from his argument:

2011's pool of female talent is terribly thin. Elite female fighters have few worthy opponents, forcing them to settle with anyone willing to take them on. In June of 2010, Jan Finney, with a record of 8-7, fought Cristiane "Cyborg" Santos, a brawler with a 9-1 record, for the Strikeforce Featherweight

Championship. These herky-jerky matches guaranteed the division would be a meat-grinder, with elite women decimating the less experienced. It isn't just a matter of integrity, but safety too.

Fast forward to August 2012. Ronda Rousey gets a call by Dana White's secretary. She is asked to attend a dinner organized by the UFC. Dana White is rumored to attend, along with top UFC brass. It has only been two weeks since her successful title defense against Kaufman. With heresy suggesting Strikeforce is on its last legs, Rousey expects a farewell party.

The meeting place is Mr. Chow's — still White's favorite restaurant. The plans are to have dinner and head to a luxury suite for the premier episode of *Sons of Anarchy* (Not being much of a TV buff, Ronda Netflixes the show in case White quizzes her on it. None of that would matter).

A limo picks Ronda up and brings her to the entrance of Mr. Chow's. She is nervous about meeting White and his UFC acolytes. A large entourage of fitted suits watches her closely as the hostess brings her to an empty seat reserved for her right across from White.

They pop open wine and dig into grilled shrimp, chicken skewers, and Mr. Chow's signature noodles. The service is not like any Ronda has experienced, the waiters and waitresses fully aware of White's reputation as a generous tipper, known for leaving as much as $10,000 in gratuities in one night.

They pass drinks. Spirits are high, but Ronda's imagination is left to wonder what it's all about.

"Do you know what's special about this restaurant?" White says to her over a plate of egg rolls and rice.

"No," Rousey responds.

"About a year ago *TMZ* stopped me outside this restaurant and asked if the UFC would ever have a female fighter," White tells her. "I said, 'never.'"

Rousey's lips go numb.

"Well," White continues, "I brought you here to say women are going to be in the UFC," White beams. "And you're its first fighter."[lxxiii]

UFC fighters are usually signed through fax, email, and if they're really lucky, a firm handshake. When the UFC signs Rousey, it's a celebration. After watching *Sons of Anarchy* the crowd makes its way to Gladstone's in Malibu — a bar where Rousey once worked as a cocktail waitress.

There she was, sitting with Dana White and company, her former boss and coworkers waiting on her. It is all so surreal. In their conversation, White doesn't ignore the fringe benefits that Rousey has to offer, and comments straight up:

> *"Obviously she's pretty. That's the first obvious thing. No. 2 is her fighting style, which is impressive, exciting. She won the same way every time even though they knew it* [the armbar] *was coming. And then when you meet her and I mean really hang out with her, you see that personality. I don't mean this the*

wrong way but she's a guy in a girl's body. She reminded me of hanging out with any other fighter...There is no way you can meet Ronda Rousey and not be interested in seeing her fight. [lxxiv]

Dana White offers her a contract on the spot. She is now officially UFC's first female fighter.

"He delivered that shit in style,"[lxxv] Rousey says, reflecting on White's offer that night.

"Ask any tattoo artist. Let's just say that women do have a higher pain tolerance than men do."

-Ronda Rousey

Rousey vs. Carmouche

Now that Ronda is signed, the question looms regarding her first opponent. Miesha Tate is ranked as the number one contender, but she's managed only one win since her 2012 loss to Rousey and in unimpressive fashion to boot. Cristiane "Cyborg" Santos — former Strikeforce Featherweight Champion (Ronda's original weight class) — was stripped of the title for testing positive for steroids and faces a year's suspension.

The UFC considers waiting out the remaining days of Cyborg's suspension, considering that Cyborg is highly regarded as Ronda's biggest threat, but Cyborg admits coming down from Featherweight to Bantamweight the way Ronda did is physically impossible. Since the UFC only holds a single women's weight class, Cyborg chooses to sign with Invicta Fighting Championship instead, the only all-female promotion in MMA.

Who else is there? Sarah McMann is an option. She's undefeated and a 2004 Olympic silver medalist, but has yet to take on a top ten opponent. Plus, her fights thus far weren't nearly as impressive as Ronda's, having gone to decision in half of her bouts.

Then Along comes Liz Carmouche; signed by the UFC shortly after Ronda. She issues Rousey a challenge through social media, becoming the only fighter brave enough to call her out. She stalks Dana White on twitter and dedicates herself to training. Sun up and sun down, Carmouche is in the gym training; all of it tweeted or posted on Facebook for the UFC to see. She wants it bad and Ronda knows it. Ronda comments on Carmouche's tenacity during a press conference:

> "*I can't make these girls fight who don't want to fight me.* [Carmouche] *was the only one who stepped up, and it speaks a lot* [about] *her. When the other girls come around, they know where I'm at.*"[lxxvi]

Despite her persistence, Liz "Girl-Rilla" Carmouche is a hard sell. On the bright side, Carmouche is the UFC's first openly gay fighter — a headline guarantee — but she lacks the blonde bombshell look, Ronda's Olympic pedigree, or a pristine record. At 8-2 she is far from unsuccessful, but during her last six fights, Carmouche needed a combined 45 minutes to subdue her opponents while Rousey needed less than eight.

What Carmouche *does* have is fearlessness – a rare form of mental strength that can only come from putting one's life on the line. She served in the Marine Corps for five years and four months as a helicopter electrician and completed three tours of duty in Iraq. Amazingly, one of the main reasons she joined the service was to experience the thrill of a real combat situation, something she accomplished during her first tour of Iraq by volunteering to go on patrols outside the wire.

Liz Carmouche. Photographer unknown.

White holds off his decision until December the eighth of 2012 He stands at the podium of *UFC on Fox 5: Henderson vs. Diaz* post-fight press conference and officially announces the Ronda Rousey vs. Liz Carmouche fight is on, set to take place less than two months later, at *UFC 157*.

Carmouche's constant campaigning won the day. For Ronda, her new opponent presents a unique problem — While Ronda's trash-talk and cold demeanor intimidated her past opponents, Carmouche's combat experience makes her impervious to fear. Like Brian Stann and other UFC war vets, seasoned soldiers have stared death in the face, making anything else — including hand-to-hand combat in front of thousands of spectators — tame in comparison.

The media obligations for both fighters begin immediately, and are extremely demanding. The

UFC expects Carmouche to pry her way into the consciousness of MMA fans, while Rousey must demonstrate that the tough, take-no-prisoners champion can handle the tirade of media frenzy. Strikeforce was one thing, but being in the UFC brings media obligations to a whole new level.

*UFC Primetim*e films Rousey and Carmouche's every move. A camera crew once again enters Rousey's Venice home.

Christmas ornaments and tennis balls hang from the ceiling of every room. She doesn't trust herself to stay disciplined, so she hangs these training tools as reminder to practice her boxing and head movement. Every time she passes them, she works her boxing technique.

Ronda's teenage half-sister, Julia, watches from off camera as Rousey demonstrates her boxing skills for *Primetime'*s *camera*. Julia is the spitting image of Ronda minus the blonde hair. She takes after Ronda's personality too, coming across as shy and reserved, just like her half-sister at that age.

They grab their wet-gear and skim-boards and walk the few short blocks to the beach. Ronda's athleticism shines. Her balance and control of the board looks effortless despite the pull of the strong tide. The afternoon sun makes her hair glow. Watching her move in the ocean is like observing a cat in the jungle — equally graceful and dangerous.

Back at Ronda's, they hang out in the kitchen. There seems to be a maternal quality about their relationship. Ronda feels it is her duty to set a good example:

"I had a lot of self-esteem issues when I was a kid. And...I never want her to beat herself up or criticize herself the way that I did... Did you already eat?"^{lxxvii}

Julia responds:

"Umm... A lot of chips,"

"That's not food," Ronda argues.

Fight day approaches. Rousey is doing the last thing you would expect her in training — relaxing in a sauna while drinking Heineken. But that's only the gist of it — she's actually using the same rejuvenation process that Fedor Emelianenko and many Russian fighters used during their training camp, a method she's picked up from her Armenian trainer.

It's called Banya. Ronda lies on the bench inside a sauna while her trainer takes two bunches of oak branches in either hand. Branches are fluffed then brushed against Ronda's back — this releases the sap, allowing the skin to absorb it. Like a hard massage, the scrapping from the twigs is uncomfortable at first, but soon relaxation sets in and recovery (in theory) quickens. What the Heineken has to do with Banya rejuvenation isn't clear, but is seems to be working.

One week out — the long days of training, interviews and promos have exhausted Ronda, but she is too amped to really feel it. She is bombarded with repeated questions regarding an unexpected move by the UFC —when Strikeforce folded, Ronda signed the UFC contract and Dana White traded her Strikeforce belt in for a UFC one, making her the female UFC champion without having fought in the organization. During the pre-fight press conference, Ronda expresses her disagreement with White's decision:

> *"All the people think that I don't deserve this belt, that I didn't earn it...I partially agree with them. I won't consider myself UFC champion until I win the belt inside the Octagon."[lxxviii]*

The fight is now days away. Rousey is cutting weight again, coming in at 141 pounds or six pounds over. Her last few sessions are less intense, allowing her body a chance to recover so that she peaks the night of the fight. Rousey struggles with the easier workouts:

> *"I have trouble bringing it down...I'm just an aggressive person in general, so when he* [Edmond Tarverdyan] *tells me to take it easy, it doesn't really register that well with me."[lxxix]*

The next morning is Ronda's final workout. With the tunes cranked and the window down, Ronda's silky blond hair blows back as she races along Brand Boulevard. She spots a sedan on her left trying to gun it past her.

"Are you trying to race me, woman?" Ronda screams at the driver. She blows past the car and speeds ahead. She pulls into Glendale Fighting Club, grabs her duffel bag of gear and enters the gym one last time.

A friend ties Ronda's hair up in two tight buns. Ronda throws on a pair of Monster over-ear headphones and warms up on the elliptical. When Tarverdyan is ready, they jump into the ring and shadowbox, running through the combos and counters they've practiced countless times already. Forty minutes later, Ronda packs up and heads back to Oakland for the night.

"I know that all the hard work is done. I feel relief and intense focus."[lxxx]

Fast forward to February 21 — two days out. Ronda and Liz are now in Anaheim, handling last minute press obligations. They attend the pre-fight press conference and are generally respectful of each other. The only thing strange is Rousey's refusal to carry or touch her UFC belt more than she has to. When the press conference is finished, Rousey and Carmouche stand face-to-face for the mandatory stare-down. Rousey leaves the belt on the conference table, but Dana White grabs it and insists she wear it. As White drapes the belt around her shoulder just in time for the press to shower the combatants with camera flashes, Ronda looks displeased.

24 hours later, the weigh-in event is held at Anaheim's Honda Center. A large stage, lighting, backdrop, and towering speakers are setup in front of a packed audience and press. UFC crew enters through the side-stage curtains carrying the official scale. The crowd roars as the crew position it center-stage. Hard rock music blares and lights strobe to signal the start of the show.

Mike Goldberg, UFC color commentator, calls out fighters one by one, each of them taking their turn on the scale while medical staff observe and call out their official weight. For non-title bouts, fighters are given a one-pound leeway. For example, if fighters compete in the lightweight division, with a weight limit of 155 pounds, fighters can weigh in at 156 without penalty (Rousey and Carmouche must weigh in on the money. If either of them comes in overweight, the bout is demoted to a non-title bout). Overweight fighters must forfeit 20% their purse to their opponent. Fighters with multiple infractions are removed from UFC's roster.

When the Champ Can't Make Weight

It's rare, but it happens. For the challenger, it hardly seems fair that a champ missing weight is ostensibly rewarded, their title no longer on the line. Sure, the champion is still obliged to give up 20% of their purse, and the challenger has the option to cancel and reschedule the fight, but with the relatively low pay that UFC non-title holders receive, coupled with the high cost of training camps, challengers fight to pay the bills. Additionally, a canceled main event might mean the entire card is scrapped, placing the guilt on the challenger when the entire roster loses their paycheck.

At *World Extreme Cagefighting 36* (WEC), Chael Sonnen was scheduled to fight defending middleweight champ Paulo Filho. Filho weighed in at 189, four pounds over the middleweight limit. Sonnen agreed to fight on even though the belt was no longer up for grabs. He won via unanimous decision. Filho pledged to mail the belt to Sonnen and schedule a rematch, but when WEC was unexpectedly absorbed by the UFC less than a month later, Filho remained the last official WEC middleweight champion.(According to Sonnen, Filho *did* mail the WEC belt.)

Liz Carmouche is ready to weigh-in. She enters from backstage looking happy and relaxed. She waves to the onlookers and they give a respectful applause, but it's obvious who they really came to see. Carmouche removes her gray hoodie and Throwdown t-shirt revealing a black and red Throwdown sports bra beneath. Her fight camp has transformed her — her body looks carved out of granite, her skin bronze from afternoon runs in the San Diego sun. Carmouche's sculpted abs gleam as cameras flash from the press box. It's clear she's had the best training camp of her life.

Carmouche jumps on the scale and medical staff read the official weight. Surprisingly, she weighs a pound and a half under the 135 limit, an indication that Carmouche's frame is too small for bantamweight. Carmouche steps off, walks to the right of the stage and stands awaiting the champion. Goldberg calls Ronda out and she enters through the side curtain.

The crowd loses it. She manages a quick smile for the audience, but her grin fades into a cold and focused stare. She walks onstage, removes her blue jeans and black hoodie, revealing a black UFC sports bra and matching underwear. It is only the second time in UFC history that the company has sponsored its own fighter. It is clear who the company wants to win.

Rousey weighs in a pound heavier than Carmouche, but still within the 135 limit. Rousey's trademark intensity is in full swing now — she jumps off the scale and stalks her opponent, meeting her face-to-face for the final stare-down before the bout. Rousey is respectful enough not to start a physical altercation then and there, a common problem at UFC weigh-ins, but it's clear that Rousey feels a healthy amount of disdain for any woman looking to take her on. "No one has a right to beat you," her mom used to say before Ronda's judo tournaments. It seems Ronda took the advice to heart. But Rousey's larger frame and menacing stare aren't having an effect. The Iraq War veteran looks unperturbed.

The next evening, the crowd pours into the Honda Center. *UFC 157* is a sellout — 13,257 tickets sold, raking in a $1,350,191 at the gate, setting a new record for world's largest PPV draw headlined by women.

Carmouche waits in the Octagon while Rousey stands outside the cage door as Jacob "Stitch" Duran, UFC's premiere cutman, applies Vaseline to Ronda's face. Another official searches for contraband then gives the go-ahead to enter the cage. Ronda darts up the Octagon steps and enters. The crowd roars and Ronda darts to her corner. She is ready.

The fighters meet in the middle, referee John McCarthy stipulates the rules, they touch gloves and return to their respective corners. The bell sounds. No time is wasted — Rousey and Carmouche dash for the center of the Octagon. They circle each other briefly, then Rousey rushes in, immediately looking for a judo throw. Carmouche defends it, but eats an uppercut to the body. Carmouche crouches down and Rousey stands above her. Rousey tries to pin one of Carmouche's arms down, but the former Marine sneaks around and leaps on Rousey's back. Rousey stands up, but Carmouche hangs on and manages to hook her legs around Rousey's waist. She is now piggybacking Rousey in an upright position, an extremely vulnerable place for Rousey or any MMA fighter to be in. Carmouche wraps her arms around Ronda's neck, looking for a rear naked choke.

This is by far the most trouble Ronda has been in during her MMA career. But, she keeps her chin down, preventing Carmouche from wrapping her forearms around her neck and asphyxiating her. Regardless, Carmouche has other options — she wraps her arm tightly over Rousey's face and cranks Rousey's head to the side. Carmouche's grip tightens and Rousey's neck twists painfully. Ronda looks ready to tap.

Carmouche holds the crank until Rousey bends over and shakes the challenger off. Carmouche falls to her back and Rousey stands above Carmouche now, landing shots to the midsection before dropping down to engage her on the ground. She controls Carmouche's head and arms and peppers her with short lefts. 90 seconds remain in the first round.

Carmouche counterattacks with another submission — an inverted triangle — but Rousey slips out. Carmouche is now vulnerable to Rousey's trademark submission, and it doesn't take long for Rousey to utilize it. She grabs at Carmouche's arm, taking her time with it; ensuring one armbar is all it will take. Carmouche uses her free arm to defend the armbar by clasping down with all her might. Carmouche uses her legs to push Rousey off, but she can't seem to free herself completely. Less than fifteen seconds remain.

Rousey secures her grip and cranks the arm back. Carmouche grimaces, tries to fight the pain, but taps out with only 11 seconds left in round one. The ref jumps in and separates them. Carmouche appears stunned, but she quickly gets to her feet and cracks a smile, waving to the crowd and looking content with her performance. Never has any UFC competitor been so gracious in defeat.

In a post-fight interview with Ariel Helwani, He asks Ronda if she has time to stop and bask in her success now that her first UFC title defense is over.

> *"Yes, I'm very happy right now. I can't wait to see my mom and eat Buffalo wings."*[lxxxi]

Ronda is now content with calling herself an undisputed UFC champion and she feels weightless, the high expectations demanded from her by her coaches and the company itself, now met. When news crews demand post-fight interviews, she apologizes and admits she is far too exhausted to hold a conversation. In all her years of competition, she's never felt so drained.

When Ronda sleeps that night, she sleeps like the dead, only to wake up the following morning to a startling realization — despite the successful title defense, the crowd-pleasing performance, and the monster paycheck — Ronda is depressed.

She can't remember most of the fight. There are tiny snippets in her mind, but her mind feels lost in a haze. It's hard to pinpoint why. A comedown? — weeks of preparation and exposure keeping her endorphins surging only for it to drop off when there's no one to fight? Maybe she is drained mentally, from the demands of always being *on* — keeping sharp for the bombardment of cameras, questions, meet-and-greets, talk shows, hard workouts and new techniques. There was nothing left of her and no impending fight to keep her adrenaline spiked. Sure, the post-fight press would come knocking, but the intensity of her life is now a fraction of what it was during preparation.

She feels guilty about being dissatisfied. Why isn't she grateful? During moments like these, she feels like an egomaniac. Why does she need to be the center of attention all the time? The thoughts play with her self-esteem.

"If I were someone else...Would I even want to be friends with me?"

With no immediate goal to accomplish or stress about, Rousey's body finds a way to do it for her. She wakes some mornings in a panic, her heart racing as she obsesses over things — comments she made, a question to the media she regrets answering. Ronda distracts herself with movies and junk food. She's a perfectionist. Nothing is ever good enough.

I either get men coming up to me like, "Oh, my God, baby, I love you!" or else they're too shy to approach me. Can I get just a little in between?

— Ronda Rousey

The Future

UFC 157 puts to rest any doubts regarding women's place in the UFC and mixed martial arts. But no fight, no matter how entertaining, is successful without profit. To ensure *UFC 157* made money, the UFC went frenzy, a fact Liz and Ronda can account for. The hard work paid off

Fans bought *UFC 157* on PPV 500,000 times, earning over $31 000 000 in sales, making it the sixth largest moneymaker for the UFC in 2012 and 2013 and outselling Laila Ali vs. Jackie Frazier five-to-one.[lxxxii] Ronda's debut also beat other cards headlined by tenured UFC champions including Jon Jones, Anderson Silva, Benson Henderson, Jose Aldo, and Frankie Edgar. She is now the fourth largest PPV draw in the UFC after just one showing.

Ronda's post-fight lull doesn't last. She embraces the downtime and the relatively relaxed media attention. Several days after her win, she sits down with Mike Tyson on *Good Day LA*. Tyson takes the opportunity to warn her about the perils of fame and fortune. He is brutally honest, telling her that he first lost the joy of competing in 1986 at age 20, after he won the world title. Part of Tyson's problem, he admits, was the unrealistic expectations he put on himself. Tyson says with a laugh:

> *"I want(ed) to be a god. I'm a dreamer. I have delusions of grandeur,"* [lxxxiii]

Like Ronda, kids bullied Tyson as a child, leading to struggles with self-esteem he still battles with today. After his trainer, Cus D'Amato, died of Pneumonia in 1985, Tyson spiraled out of control. He took hard drugs, spent his fortune on hookers, strippers and extravagant purchases, and ended up in prison for statutory rape in 1992. He made a comeback three years later, but he was never the same boxer.

When host Steve Edwards asked Tyson if he has any advice for the up-and-coming Rousey, Tyson responds:

> *"Stick with your mom and a good lawyer."[lxxxiv]*

Rousey seems to be handling the pressures of fame with ease so far. But women in the UFC have yet to earn their tenure. Even after signing Rousey in August of 2012, Dana White spoke to the media after *UFC 154*:

> *"I'm trying this whole women's thing out..."*

What will happen after the honeymoon phase of the women's division fizzles out; when the novelty and freshness are gone? Will people lose interest? Will cards headlined by women other than Ronda Rousey have drawing power? What if Rousey loses or suffers an injury? What if she seeks a career in Hollywood?

Ronda's dedication to training is undeniable, but she is in a similar position as Gina Carano was in 2010. She has the looks, talent, and personality fit for life outside the cage. Will she follow in Carano's footsteps? Will she fight on if/when she suffers a tough loss?

Ronda has movie offers already, including a role in the sequel to Hollywood blockbuster, *The Hunger Games*. In late February 2013, she signed with WME talent agency, a company whose clientele include Denzel Washington, Ben Stiller, Tina Fey, and Steve Carell.

Jonathan Snowden, a lead writer for Bleacherreport.com, in his *Bold Predictions* segment, has a lot to say about Rousey's future. By what he sees in the Octagon, he predicts she will continue to dominate in her weight class, grappling and submitting opponents until it becomes monotonous.

> *"In two years, Ronda Rousey will not be a full-time UFC fighter...Rousey is too big for the sport. Even before UFC 157, Rousey was taking offers from big time Hollywood producers, big time Hollywood directors. Ronda Rousey's future isn't in the cage; it's on the silver screen."[lxxxv]*

One look at the Internet Movie Database (imdb.com) shows Rousey taking part in a TV series and two documentaries in 2013 and 2014, including a special detailing her personal life called *Through my Father's Eyes*, due out June 2013. The world awaits her.

"There's no amount of press that can save these girls from me"
— Ronda Rousey

The Biggest Threat

Women's MMA is only in its infancy — a monsoon of tough, capable female fighters are about to rain in from the amateur division. Among these up-and-comers is Sarah McMann, a fellow Olympic medalist who won silver in women's freestyle wrestling in 2004. Like Rousey, she holds an undefeated record (7-0), and took a first round submission win against Sheila Gaff in her UFC debut. To date, no other discipline has ensured success in MMA more than a strong wrestling background and with an Olympic medal; McMann is the most accomplished wrestler ever to step into the cage.

According to Dave Camarillo, a judo and jiu jitsu black belt and former coach at one of MMA's top gyms, he sees a lot of holes in Rousey's game despite her success. Some of her technique is still based on judo rules, leaving her open to submissions in MMA, like in the case where she was almost neck-cranked by Liz Carmouche. When Luke Thomas of MMAFighting.com asked him to lay out the blueprint to beat Ronda, he replied:

> *"Just look at her fight. The fight's almost always over when she gets the clinch and takes the opponent down, gets her to where she wants her, finishes her. So, you gotta out-clinch her. Yeah, good footwork would be awesome, but you're going to get in the clinch. Well, you've gotta out-clinch her. You have to break free, get her*

tired. Once she's tired, who knows what's going to happen? A lot of fighters who keep winning, they get punched in the face and then the second that doubt enters the mind, that's the experience." lxxxvi

And Next Up...

Ronda is scheduled to start filming *The Ultimate Fighter 18* in the summer of 2013, the first of the reality series to feature female fighters. She will coach a team of fighters against Cat Zingano, another undefeated UFC competitor who earned her spot on the show by taking out Miesha Tate at *TUF 17*. Zingano will be the first opponent to match Ronda in strength and size.

In late May 2013, Black House MMA announced Zingano as a new member of their team. Black House is by far the most exclusive and secretive elite gym in mixed martial arts. It is home to UFC's best — Rodrigo and Rogerio Nogueira, Glover Teixeira, Lyoto Machida, and the greatest pound-for-pound fighter of all time, UFC middleweight champion Anderson Silva. There's no better gym to train for a bout, making Rousey vs. Zingano a surefire hit.

(Update for June 01, 2013: Due to serious knee injury, Zingano is out of The Ultimate Fighter and replaced by Meisha Tate. Although Tate lost to Zingano, dropping her bid to coach on TUF, Tate dominated the first two rounds of the Zingano fight

only to lose by referee stoppage in the third; a
stoppage many UFC alumni felt was too early.)

"You've gotta worry MOST about the PRETTY fighters. Because they obviously get hit the LEAST."

— Ronda Rousey

PART IV: EPILOGUE

MMA: Sport or Entertainment?

Unlike mainstream sports, MMA has no official standings to determine who fighters should be matched up against, or which fighter deserves the next title shot. All too often, contenders with superior records are passed over in favor of contenders with more ticket sale potential.

Brock Lesnar, for example, earned a UFC heavyweight title shot in 2008 after only one win and one loss. His popularity as a former WWE superstar pushed him ahead of more deserving fighters like Shane Carwin, who was 9-0 at the time.

Should MMA allow fighters who are less deserving cut in line for the sake of profit even if it's what fans want to see? What will happen to the sport's legitimacy if personality and trash-talk take precedence over skill and athleticism?

Chael Sonnen, arguably the most quotable fighter since Muhammad Ali, talked his way into a light-heavyweight title shot in 2013 against Jon Jones, even when Chael was coming off a loss for the middleweight championship and did not compete in the light-heavyweight division since 2005. Tickets sold well, but Sonnen was decimated by the much larger, more talented Jones.

Bellator Fighting Championship has implemented tournaments as a surefire way to give successful fighters the opportunities they deserve and avoid the pitfalls of becoming a spectator sport. Bellator tournaments are sudden death with the tournament winner given an automatic shot at the title.

The argument against this type of tournament is that fans don't get to watch the fights they really want to see. In addition, tournament participants must fight often, sometimes with as little as a month to heal from previous bouts. Meanwhile, the titleholder waits on the sidelines, fighting less deserving opponents in non-title bouts to keep busy.

What is the right way promotions should handle matchmaking? Should fan entertainment and PPV buys take priority over rankings? Or should organizers find a safe middle ground?

So You Wanna Be a UFC Fighter?! : High Cost/Low Reward

Does beachside property, personal chefs, first-class airfare, and fine-dining appeal to you? Then get into real estate. Big name UFC stars, WWE pro wrestler and retired fighter Brock Lesnar in particular, make millions from their fight purse, cut of PPV sales, and sponsorship deals. The rest of the fighters, one of Lesnar's opponents for instance, Shane Carwin, make a fraction of Lesnar's earnings. Carwin earned a measly $40,000 in his bout against Lesnar, despite steamrolling his way up the heavyweight ranks, remaining undefeated at 12-0, and ending all his fights by submission, TKO, or KO in the first round.

New Contender: Rise of the Transgender Fighter

Cage fighting already has a bad reputation for dabbling into a freak-show spectacle. Steroid ridden athletes are still caught on a regular basis and facetious trash-talking more akin to professional wrestling is used to inflate the number of tickets sold.

Then comes Fallon Fox, MMA's first transgender contender.

Fox was born in Toledo Ohio to religious, conservative parents. As of 2013 she is 37 years old, but her exact birth date (as of early 2013) has not been publicly released. Fox remembers feeling gender confused as early as six, but continued her life as a heterosexual male, even having a child and marrying at the age of 20.

Fox joined the Navy and later attended the University of Toledo, but the psychological issues that came with her gender confusion made studying impossible and so she dropped out. Fox moved to Chicago with her daughter and worked as a truck driver while saving for gender reassignment surgery.

The most advanced surgical procedures regarding reassignment surgery are located in Bangkok, Thailand. Fox, now 30, made the trip and underwent reassignment — breast augmentation, a hair transplant and most importantly, genital reassignment. She began hormone supplement therapy to reduce her testosterone and increase estrogen.

The mixed martial arts athletic commission recognizes a transgender person\s newly assigned sex. In the eyes of the commission, Fox is 100% female. But issues remain

First let's look at Fallon's record. As of May 2013, she has only one amateur bout and three pro bouts, but she has dominated her opponents quite severely so far, winning all her fights in the first round, including a TKO and KO within the first two minutes except her most recent which lasted three rounds with Fox winning by submission. Watching her fights elicits a sudden observation — Fox's technique needs work, but her strength is first-rate. In other words, she is manhandling these women (pun intended).

The obvious question remains – does Fox's original gender give her an unfair advantage? Science points to – yes.

The male and female bodies are very similar until male puberty hits. Since Fallon had reassignment surgery post-puberty, she went through the testosterone surge that all young boys experience. With that comes increased bone density, stronger ligaments, increased aggression, muscle mass, and better endurance. Her hormonal supplements have reduced the impact that puberty has had on her body, but it has not been fully reversed.

Dr. **Ramona Krutzik, M.D,** certified endocrinologist, in an interview with bloodyelbow.com, has this to say about Fallon's unfair advantage:

> *"When pitted against an average female, I would say that there were probably some advantages that the hormonal blockade and subsequent replacement can't take away 100%, simply because she lived so much of her life as a male, and developed fully as such.* "[lxxxvii]

Ronda Rousey, as always, doesn't shy away from making her opinion known.

> *"She can try hormones, chop her pecker off, but it's still the same bone structure a man has...It's an advantage. I don't think it's fair."*[lxxxviii]

Sex Appeal vs. Athleticism

It is November 12, 2012 and Ronda Rousey appears on the *Jim Rome Show* during his "Ten Questions" segment. With a tousled head of hair and a megawatt smile, the last thing she looks like is a UFC fighter. But at a second glance, the signs of hard sparring are apparent. Her short skirt does little to cover the massive bruise on her right thigh and a welt on the left side of her forehead.

Rome and Rousey discuss the fight game — how throwing the perfect punch can be likened to hitting a ball with the sweet spot of a bat. And they discuss the importance of a healthy diet in the recovery process of a fighter. But one question will dominate the MMA headlines the following morning, and it has nothing to do with her technique or diet.

"Some boxers abstain from sex up to six weeks before the fight," Rome asks Rousey. "What is your philosophy on this [in regards to women MMA fighters]?"

> *"For girls, it raises your testosterone so I try to have as much sex as possible."*

Critiques of Rousey's quick rise to the top contribute her success to her looks just as much if not more than her talent as a fighter. In a separate interview, Rousey's mother is asked whether she is comfortable with her daughter being a sex symbol. She responds:

"Honestly, she doesn't even have a boyfriend," she tells the *Orange County Register. "We're very*

Catholic. I think some of what Ronda says is kind of dialed up."

According to Rousey, since becoming a symbol for MMA, her sex life has never been so lacking:

> *"Since I'm single, obviously all my relationships have had a 100-percent fail rate to this point. I need somebody who's very confident and trusting because I hang out with a bunch of guys all day long."*

She admits the sex appeal thing is a facade, used to draw attention from the media. It equates to larger fights with more PPV buys. For every buy, she is given a percentage, but looks alone don't pay the bills :

> *" If I looked the way I do and didn't fight, no one would know who I was at all. Looks depend on every single career out there. If I were to give a board presentation, would I do it in my pajamas? No, I'd put on a pencil skirt and some makeup...Even with men, they get paid more when they're taller."*

About the Author

Matt Demers hails from Windsor, Ontario. He has published everything from fitness books, comedic shorts, horror anthologies, and science fiction. He has written articles for MMArecruiter.com, The Bleacher Report and AZCentral, LiveStrong, TheNest, and many more. He hopes that Ronda will find this biography agreeable, lest he end up like balgren.

Contact Matt via email:
MATT.DEMERS@HOTMAIL.COM

Bibliography

Ain, Morty. "Ronda Rousey in Nothing but A smile." *ESPN*. ESPN, 11 July 2012. Web. 30 May 2013. http://espn.go.com/mma/story/_/id/8122712/mma-champ-ronda-rousey-poses-naked-2012-body-issue-espn-magazine?src=mobile.

Bloom, J. D. "Tachypsychia." *Dictionary of Hallucinations*. Academic Dictionaries and Encyclopedias, 2010. Web. 31 May 2013. http://hallucinations.enacademic.com/1835/tachypsychia.

Bold Predictions for UFC Star Ronda Rousey's Future. By Jonathan Snowden. *Bleacher Report*. Turner Broadcasting System, 7 Mar. 2013. Web. 31 May 2013. http://bleacherreport.com/articles/1558339-bold-predictions-for-ufc-star-ronda-rouseys-future.

Chiappetta, Mike. "Ronda Rousey on Miesha Tate: 'I Don't Think She's Better Than Me In Any Category'" *MMA Fighting*. SB Nation, 2011. Web. 31 May 2013. http://www.mmafighting.com/2011/11/21/ronda-rousey-on-miesha-tate-i-dont-think-shes-better-than-me.

Cordain, Loren. "Getting Started with the Paleo Diet." *The Paleo Diet*. N.p., n.d. Web. 31 May 2013.

http://thepaleodiet.com/getting-started-with-the-paleo-diet/ .

Cruz, Jason. "UFC 157: Payout Perspective." *MMAPayout.com*. N.p., 25 Feb. 2013. Web. 31 May 2013. http://mmapayout.com/2013/02/ufc-157-payout-perspective/.

Dana White -- Women Will Never Fight in The UFC. Prod. TMZ. *YouTube*. Google, 19 Jan. 2011. Web. http://www.youtube.com/watch?v=I4X6cUOQv6w.

"Dan Le Batard's Highly Questionable"" Interview by Dan Le Batard and Ronda Rousey.*YouTube*. Google, 2012. Web. 30 May 2013. http://www.youtube.com/watch?feature=player_embedded&v=ksGYlQBFMXs.

Gerbasi, Thomas. "Ronda Rousey: The Queen's Reign Begins." *UFC.com*. Zuffa, 22 Feb. 2013. Web. 31 May 2013. http://www.ufc.ca/news/Ronda-Rousey-The-Queens-Reign-Begins.

Good Day LA. KTTV. Los Angeles, California, 8 Mar. 2013. Television.

Gross, Josh. "Ronda Rousey Finds Time, Energy for Charity." Web log post. *ESPN Mixed Martial Arts Blog*. ESPN, 11 Mar. 2013. Web. 31 May 2013. http://espn.go.com/blog/mma/post/_/id/17068/ronda-rousey-finds-time-energy-for-charity.

Erickson, Matt. "Ronda Rousey Meets Liz Carmouche in First UFC Women's Title Fight at UFC 157." *Ronda Rousey Meets Liz Carmouche in First UFC Women's Title Fight at UFC 157*. MMA Junkie, 6 Dec. 2012. Web. 31 May 2013. http://www.mmajunkie.com/news/2012/12/ronda-rousey-meets-liz-carmouche-in-first-ufc-womens-title-fight-at-ufc-157.

Fowlkes, Ben. "Miesha Tate and Ronda Rousey Have Our Attention, But Does It Matter How They Got It?" *MMA Fighting*. SB Nation, 21 Feb. 2012. Web. 31 May 2013. http://www.mmafighting.com/2012/2/21/2814890/miesha-tate-and-ronda-rousey-have-our-attention-but-does-it-matter.

Hendricks, Maggie. "Ronda Rousey Has a History of Using Her Voice to Make Change." Web log post. *Yahoo Sports Canada*. Yahoo, 1 Mar. 2012. Web. 30 May 2013. http://ca.sports.yahoo.com/blogs/mma-cagewriter/ronda-rousey-history-using-her-voice-change-151925991.html.

Holland, Jesse. "Miesha Tate Arm Injury Update: 'I Basically Tore Everything, but I'll Be Back Stronger than Ever." *MMAmania.com*. SB Nation, 4 May 2012. Web. 31 May 2013. http://www.mmamania.com/2012/5/4/2998793/miesha-tate-arm-injury-update-ronda-rousey-strikeforce-ufc-video.

Judo - About." *London2012.com*. London 2012 Olympic and Paralympic Games, n.d. Web. 30 May 2013. http://www.london2012.com/judo/about.

Kostopanagiotou, Georgia, Ioanna Siafaka, Constantinos Sikiotis, and Vassilios Smyrniotis. "Result Filters." *Journal of Clinical Anesthesia* 16.6 (2004): 458-60.*National Center for Biotechnology Information.* U.S. National Library of Medicine, 2004. Web. 30 May 2013. http://www.ncbi.nlm.nih.gov/pubmed/21699652

Krutzik, Ramona, Dr. "Dr. Ramona Krutzik, M.D. Discusses Possible Advantages Fallon Fox May Have." Interview by Steph Daniels. *Bloody Elbow*. SB Nation, 20 Mar. 2013. Web. 31 May 2013. http://www.bloodyelbow.com/2013/3/20/4128658/dr-ramona-krutzik-endocrinologist-discusses-possible-advantages-fallon-fox-has.

Mihoces, Gary. "U.S. Judo Coach Hope His Team Can Claim Medal, Grab Attention - USATODAY.com." *U.S. Judo Coach Hope His Team Can Claim Medal, Grab Attention - USATODAY.com.* USA Today, 8 Dec. 2008. Web. 30 May 2013. http://usatoday30.usatoday.com/sports/olympics/beijing/fight/2008-08-12-usa-judocoach_N.htm?csp=34.

Moore, David L. "Ronda Rousey Ready for UFC Octagon History." *USA Today*. Gannett, 2013. Web. 30 May 2013. http://www.usatoday.com/story/sports/mma/2013/02/20/ronda-rousey-ufc-mixed-martial-arts/1934113/.

Nashville, Rob. "UFC Chief Lorenzo Fertitta Talks about Buying UFC in 2001."*MMAPayout.com.* MMAPayout, 03 Mar. 2009. Web. 30 May 2013. http://mmapayout.com/2009/03/ufc-chief-lorenzo-fertitta-talks-about-buying-ufc-in-2001/

OlyMADMen, comp. "Claudia Heill." *Sports
Reference*. N.p., n.d. Web. 30 May 2013.
http://www.sports-
reference.com/olympics/athletes/he/claudia-heill-1.html.

Pugmire, Lance. "Ronda Rousey's Maverick Ways
Lead to Landmark UFC Bout." *Los Angeles Times*. Los
Angeles Times, 21 Feb. 2013. Web. 30 May 2013.
http://articles.latimes.com/2013/feb/21/sports/la-sp-
0222-ronda-rousey-20130222

Raimondi, Marc. "UFC Women's Champ Rousey
Weighs in on Transgender Fighter Controversy." *New
York Post*. NYP Holdings, 10 Apr. 2013. Web. 31 May
2013.
http://www.nypost.com/p/blogs/the_main_event/ufc_wo
men_champ_weighs_in_on_transgender_3x7mCaaXn27
HVq1QtuO5lN#axzz2UuYrdpuI.

Rogan, Joe. "Joe Rogan LIVE Podcast #168." Video
blog post. *YouTube*. The Joe Rogan Experience, 21 Dec.
2011. Web. 31 May 2013.
http://www.youtube.com/watch?v=fkFQdKpoQnQ.

Ronda Rousey - Sports Illustrated. Prod. Clear Cut
Digital. *YouTube*. Sports Illustrated, 16 Mar. 2012. Web.
31 May 2013.
http://www.youtube.com/watch?v=kTBgc2pw_bs.

Ronda Rousey's Trip to the 209. Prod. Middle Easy
TV. *YouTube*. Throwdown, 10 May 2012. Web. 31 May

2013.
http://www.youtube.com/watch?v=bh8ZWWN8pNQ.

Rousey, Ronda. "Ronda Rousey Blog: Over Coming
Obstacles" *SportsNet*. Rogers Media, 20 Feb. 2010.
Web. 30 May 2013.
http://www.sportsnet.ca/mma/ufc/ronda-rousey-blog-
overcoming-obstacles/

Rousey, Ronda. "Interview with "Rowdy" Ronda
Rousey." Interview by Chad Morrison. Web log
post. *Akari Judo Blog*. Akari Judo Club, 26 July 2011.
Web. 30 May 2013.
http://blog.akarijudo.com/2011/07/interview-with-ronda-
rowdy-rousey.html

Rousey, Ronda. ""Livin' the Vida Lazy"." Web log
Post. *Ronda Rousey (dot net!): Following the judo Life
— from a blonder perspective.* N.p., n.d. Web.

Rousey, Ronda. "Ronda Rousey Blog: My Pampered
Life?" *SportsNet*. Rogers Media, 28 Feb. 2012. Web. 30
May 2013. http://www.sportsnet.ca/mma/ufc/ronda-
rousey-blog-my-pampered-life.

Rousey, Ronda. "Ronda Rousey Tells Us in Detail
What It Feels like to Tear Apart an Arm." Interview by
LayzieTheSavage. *YouTube*. Middle Easy TV, 30 Sept.
2012. Web. 30 May 2013.
http://www.youtube.com/watch?feature=player_embedd
ed&v=LniOgTmoejI.

Rousey, Ronda. "Dan Le Batard's Highly Questionable"" Interview by Dan Le Batard. *YouTube*. ESPN, 2012. Web. 30 May 2013. http://www.youtube.com/watch?feature=player_embedded&v=ksGYlQBFMXs.

Rousey, Ronda. "Women's UFC Star Ronda Rousey, Unplugged." Interview by Sean Greggory. Web log post. *Time Sports*. Time, 2013. Web. http://keepingscore.blogs.time.com/2013/02/22/womens-ufc-star-ronda-rousey-unplugged.

'Rowdy Ronda' Rousey Uses Elbow-breaking Signature Move to Win Historic Women's Ultimate Fighting Championships Debut." *Mail Online*. Daily Mail Reporter, 2013. Web. 31 May 2013. http://www.dailymail.co.uk/news/article-2284250/Ronda-Rousey-fight-Rowdy-Ronda-uses-elbow-breaking-signature-wins-historic-womens-Ultimate-Fighting-Championships-debut.html.

Samano, Simon. "MMA Star Ronda Rousey Blasts Michael Phelps for Being a Jerk." *USA Today*. Gannett, 21 July 2012. Web. 30 May 2013. http://content.usatoday.com/communities/gameon/post/2012/07/mma-star-ronda-rousey-blasts-michael-phelps-for-being-a-jerk/1.

Silicon Valley Sports Entertainment, prod. "Strikeforce: Tate vs. Rousey." *Strikeforce*. Showtime. 3 Mar. 2012. Television.

Smith, Micahel D. "Judo Olympian Ronda Rousey Uses Her Blog to Accuse an Official of Molesting Athletes." *AOL News*. AOL, 2008. Web. 30 May 2013. http://www.aolnews.com/2008/06/25/judo-olympian-ronda-rousey-uses-her-blog-to-accuse-an-official-o.

Snowden, Jonathan. "The Gentle Way: Strikeforce Champion Ronda Rousey and the Birth of a Judo Star." *Bleacher Report*. Turner Broadcasting System, 6 Apr. 2012. Web. 30 May 2013. http://bleacherreport.com/articles/1134250-the-gentle-way-strikeforce-champion-ronda-rousey-and-the-birth-of-a-judo-star.

Spike TV, prod. *MMA Uncensored Live*. N.d. *YouTube*. Google, 2 Mar. 2012. Web. 31 May 2013. http://www.youtube.com/watch?v=Uqu0s1ynQss.

Strikeforce, prod. "Showtime - All Access: Ronda Rousey." *All Access*. Showtime. 8 Aug. 2012. Television.

Thamel, Pete. "A Journey Out of Pain, Through Judo." *The New York Times*. The New York Times, 12 Aug. 2008. Web. 30 May 2013. http://www.nytimes.com/2008/08/12/sports/olympics/12judo.html?pagewanted=print.

Thomas, Luke. "Technique Talk: Dave Camarillo on Judo in MMA and the Challenge of Ronda Rousey." *MMA Fighting*. SB Nation, 2013. Web. 02 June 2013. http://www.mmafighting.com/2013/6/1/4385780/techniq

ue-talk-dave-camarillo-judo-mma-ronda-rousey-blueprint-mma-news.

Watson, Callie, and Simon Wilkinson. "One-meal-a-day Diets under the Microscope."*News.Com.Au*. News Life Media, 2013. Web. 31 May 2013. http://www.news.com.au/lifestyle/health-fitness/one-meal-a-day-diets-under-the-miscroscope/story-fneuz9ev-1226548163759.

Wetzel, Dan. "Dana White's About-face on Women's MMA Became Official One Historic Night Last August." *Yahoo! Sports*. Yahoo!, 2013. Web. 30 May 2013. http://sports.yahoo.com/news/mma--dana-white-s-about-face-on-women-s-mma-became-official-one-historic-night-last-august-045153399.html

Zuffa, prod. "UFC 157 Primetime: Rousey vs. Carmouche." *UFC Primetime*. FX, 7 Feb. 2013. Television.

[i] Nashville, Rob. "UFC Chief Lorenzo Fertitta Talks about Buying UFC in 2001."*MMAPayout.com*. MMAPayout, 03 Mar. 2009. Web. 30 May 2013. <http://mmapayout.com/2009/03/ufc-chief-lorenzo-fertitta-talks-about-buying-ufc-in-2001/>.

[ii] Rousey, Ronda. "Http://www.sportsnet.ca/mma/ufc/ronda-rousey-blog-overcoming-obstacles/." *SportsNet*. Rogers Media, 20 Feb. 2010. Web. 30 May 2013. <http://www.sportsnet.ca/mma/ufc/ronda-rousey-blog-overcoming-obstacles/>.

[iii] Pugmire, Lance. "Ronda Rousey's Maverick Ways Lead to Landmark UFC Bout." *Los Angeles Times*. Los Angeles Times, 21 Feb. 2013. Web. 30 May 2013. <http://articles.latimes.com/2013/feb/21/sports/la-sp-0222-ronda-rousey-20130222>.

[iv] Kostopanagiotou, Georgia, Ioanna Siafaka, Constantinos Sikiotis, and Vassilios Smyrniotis. "Result Filters." *Journal of Clinical Anesthesia* 16.6 (2004): 458-60. *National Center for Biotechnology Information*. U.S. National Library of Medicine, 2004. Web. 30 May 2013. <http://www.ncbi.nlm.nih.gov/pubmed/21699652>.

[v] Zuffa, prod. "UFC 157 Primetime: Rousey vs. Carmouche." *UFC Primetime*. FX, 7 Feb. 2013. Television.

[vi] Zuffa, "UFC Primetime."

[vii] Lance, "Landmark UFC Bout."

[viii] Snowden, Jonathan. "The Gentle Way: Strikeforce Champion Ronda Rousey and the Birth of a Judo Star." *Bleacher Report*. Turner Broadcasting System, 6 Apr. 2012. Web. 30 May 2013. <http://bleacherreport.com/articles/1134250-the-gentle-way-strikeforce-champion-ronda-rousey-and-the-birth-of-a-judo-star>.

[ix] Rousey, Ronda. "Ronda Rousey Tells Us in Detail What

It Feels like to Tear Apart an Arm." Interview by LayzieTheSavage. *YouTube*. Middle Easy TV, 30 Sept. 2012. Web. 30 May 2013. <http://www.youtube.com/watch?feature=player_embedded& v=LniOgTmoejI>.

[x] Rousey, Ronda. "Ronda Rousey Blog: My Pampered Life?" *SportsNet*. Rogers Media, 28 Feb. 2012. Web. 30 May 2013. <http://www.sportsnet.ca/mma/ufc/ronda-rousey-blog-my-pampered-life/>.

[xi] Rousey, "My Pampered Life?".

[xii] Rousey, Ronda. "Interview with "Rowdy" Ronda Rousey." Interview by Chad Morrison. Web log post. *Akari Judo Blog*. Akari Judo Club, 26 July 2011. Web. 30 May 2013. <http://blog.akarijudo.com/2011/07/interview-with-ronda-rowdy-rousey.html>.

[xiii] Lance, "Landmark UFC Bout."

[xiv] Rousey, Ronda. "Women's UFC Star Ronda Rousey, Unplugged." Interview by Sean Greggory. Web log post. *Time Sports*. Time, 2013. Web. <http://keepingscore.blogs.time.com/2013/02/22/womens-ufc-star-ronda-rousey-unplugged/>.

[xv] Mihoces, Gary. "U.S. Judo Coach Hope His Team Can Claim Medal, Grab Attention - USATODAY.com." *U.S. Judo Coach Hope His Team Can Claim Medal, Grab Attention - USATODAY.com*. USA Today, 8 Dec. 2008. Web. 30 May 2013. <http://usatoday30.usatoday.com/sports/olympics/beijing/fight/2008-08-12-usa-judocoach_N.htm?csp=34>.

[xvi] OlyMADMen, comp. "Claudia Heill." *Sports Reference*. N.p., n.d. Web. 30 May 2013. <http://www.sports-reference.com/olympics/athletes/he/claudia-heill-1.html>.

[xvii] Rousey, Ronda. "Dan Le Batard's Highly Questionable"" Interview by Dan Le Batard. *YouTube*. ESPN, 2012. Web. 30 May 2013. <http://www.youtube.com/watch?feature=player_embedded& v=ksGYlQBFMXs>.?feature=player_embedded&v=ksGYlQB

FMXs>.

^{xviii} Rousey. "Highly Questionable".

^{xix} Thamel, Pete. "A Journey Out of Pain, Through Judo." *The New York Times*. The New York Times, 12 Aug. 2008. Web. 02 June 2013. <http://www.nytimes.com/2008/08/12/sports/olympics/12judo.html?pagewanted=2;oref=slogin>.

^{xx} Rousey. "Unplugged".

^{xxi} Rousey, Ronda. ""Livin' the Vida Lazy"." Web log post. *Ronda Rousey (dot net!): Following the judo Life — from a blonder perspective*. N.p., n.d. Web.

^{xxii} Thamel,. "A Journey Out of Pain".

^{xxiii} "Judo - About." *London2012.com*. London 2012 Olympic and Paralympic Games, n.d. Web. 30 May 2013. <http://www.london2012.com/judo/about/>.

^{xxiv} Rousey, "Judo Life".

^{xxv} Smith, Micahel D. "Judo Olympian Ronda Rousey Uses Her Blog to Accuse an Official of Molesting Athletes." *AOL News*. AOL, 2008. Web. 30 May 2013. <http://www.aolnews.com/2008/06/25/judo-olympian-ronda-rousey-uses-her-blog-to-accuse-an-official-o/>.

^{xxvi} Hendricks, Maggie. "Ronda Rousey Has a History of Using Her Voice to Make Change." Web log post. *Yahoo Sports Canada*. Yahoo, 1 Mar. 2012. Web. 30 May 2013. <http://ca.sports.yahoo.com/blogs/mma-cagewriter/ronda-rousey-history-using-her-voice-change-151925991.html>.

^{xxvii} Rousey, "Judo Life".

^{xxviii} Rousey, "Judo Life".

^{xxix} Samano, Simon. "MMA Star Ronda Rousey Blasts Michael Phelps for Being a Jerk." *USA Today*. Gannett, 21 July 2012. Web. 30 May 2013. <http://content.usatoday.com/communities/gameon/post/2012/07/mma-star-ronda-rousey-blasts-michael-phelps-for-being-a-jerk/1>.

[xxx] Ain, Morty. "Ronda Rousey in Nothing but A smile." *ESPN*. ESPN, 11 July 2012. Web. 30 May 2013. <http://espn.go.com/mma/story/_/id/8122712/mma-champ-ronda-rousey-poses-naked-2012-body-issue-espn-magazine?src=mobile>.

[xxxi] Wetzel, Dan. "Dana White's About-face on Women's MMA Became Official One Historic Night Last August." *Yahoo! Sports*. Yahoo!, 2013. Web. 30 May 2013. <http://sports.yahoo.com/news/mma--dana-white-s-about-face-on-women-s-mma-became-official-one-historic-night-last-august-045153399.html>.

[xxxii] Zuffa, "UFC Primetime."

[xxxiii] Moore, David L. "Ronda Rousey Ready for UFC Octagon History." *USA Today*. Gannett, 2013. Web. 30 May 2013. <http://www.usatoday.com/story/sports/mma/2013/02/20/ronda-rousey-ufc-mixed-martial-arts/1934113/>.

[xxxiv] *Ronda Rousey - Sports Illustrated*. Prod. Clear Cut Digital. *YouTube*. Sports Illustrated, 16 Mar. 2012. Web. 31 May 2013. <http://www.youtube.com/watch?v=kTBgc2pw_bs>.

[xxxv] Rousey, "Judo Life".

[xxxvi] Rousey, "Judo Life".

[xxxvii] Rogan, Joe. "Joe Rogan LIVE Podcast #168." Video blog post. *YouTube*. The Joe Rogan Experience, 21 Dec. 2011. Web. 31 May 2013. <http://www.youtube.com/watch?v=fkFQdKpoQnQ>.

[xxxviii] Rogan, "Joe Rogan LIVE".

[xxxix] Rogan, "Joe Rogan LIVE".

[xl] Cordain, Loren. "Getting Started with the Paleo Diet." *The Paleo Diet*. N.p., n.d. Web. 31 May 2013. <http://thepaleodiet.com/getting-started-with-the-paleo-diet/>.

[xli] Watson, Callie, and Simon Wilkinson. "One-meal-a-day Diets under the Microscope."*News.Com.Au*. News Life Media, 2013. Web. 31 May 2013.

<http://www.news.com.au/lifestyle/health-fitness/one-meal-a-day-diets-under-the-miscroscope/story-fneuz9ev-1226548163759>.

xlii Gross, Josh. "Ronda Rousey Finds Time, Energy for Charity." Web log post. *ESPN Mixed Martial Arts Blog.* ESPN, 11 Mar. 2013. Web. 31 May 2013.
<http://espn.go.com/blog/mma/post/_/id/17068/ronda-rousey-finds-time-energy-for-charity>.

xliii Fowlkes, Ben. "Miesha Tate and Ronda Rousey Have Our Attention, But Does It Matter How They Got It?" *MMA Fighting.* SB Nation, 21 Feb. 2012. Web. 31 May 2013.
<http://www.mmafighting.com/2012/2/21/2814890/miesha-tate-and-ronda-rousey-have-our-attention-but-does-it-matter>.

xliv Chiappetta, Mike. "Ronda Rousey on Miesha Tate: 'I Don't Think She's Better Than Me In Any Category'" *MMA Fighting.* SB Nation, 2011. Web. 31 May 2013.
<http://www.mmafighting.com/2011/11/21/ronda-rousey-on-miesha-tate-i-dont-think-shes-better-than-me>.

xlv Bloom, J. D. "Tachypsychia." *Dictionary of Hallucinations.* Academic Dictionaries and Encyclopedias, 2010. Web. 31 May 2013.
<http://hallucinations.enacademic.com/1835/tachypsychia>.

xlvi Silicon Valley Sports Entertainment, prod. "Strikeforce: Tate vs. Rousey." *Strikeforce.* Showtime. 3 Mar. 2012. Television.

xlvii Silicon Valley Sports Entertainment, "Strikeforce".

xlviii Holland, Jesse. "Miesha Tate Arm Injury Update: 'I Basically Tore Everything, but I'll Be Back Stronger than Ever." *MMAmania.com.* SB Nation, 4 May 2012. Web. 31 May 2013.
<http://www.mmamania.com/2012/5/4/2998793/miesha-tate-arm-injury-update-ronda-rousey-strikeforce-ufc-video>.

xlix Gerbasi, Thomas. "Ronda Rousey: The Queen's Reign Begins." *UFC.com.* Zuffa, 22 Feb. 2013. Web. 31 May 2013.
<http://www.ufc.ca/news/Ronda-Rousey-The-Queens-Reign-Begins>.

[l] Strikeforce, prod. "Showtime - All Access: Ronda Rousey." *All Access*. Showtime. 8 Aug. 2012. Television.

[li]Rousey, "Judo Life"

[lii] Strikeforce, *All Access*.

[liii] Strikeforce, *All Access*.

[liv] Strikeforce, *All Access*.

[lv] Strikeforce, *All Access*.

[lvi] *Ronda Rousey's Trip to the 209*. Prod. Middle Easy TV. *YouTube*. Throwdown, 10 May 2012. Web. 31 May 2013. <http://www.youtube.com/watch?v=bh8ZWWN8pNQ>.

[lvii] *Trip to the 209,* Middle Easy TV

[lviii] Strikeforce, *All Access*.

[lix] Strikeforce, *All Access*.

[lx] Strikeforce, *All Access*.

[lxi] Strikeforce, *All Access*.

[lxii] Strikeforce, *All Access*.

[lxiii] Strikeforce, *All Access*.

[lxiv] Strikeforce, *All Access*.

[lxv] Strikeforce, *All Access*.

[lxvi] Strikeforce, *All Access*.

[lxvii] Strikeforce, *All Access*.

[lxviii] Strikeforce, *All Access*.

[lxix] Rousey, Ronda. "Unplugged".

[lxx] Spike TV, prod. *MMA Uncensored Live*. N.d. *YouTube*. Google, 2 Mar. 2012. Web. 31 May 2013. <http://www.youtube.com/watch?v=Uqu0s1ynQss>.

[lxxi] *Dana White -- Women Will Never Fight in The UFC*. Prod. TMZ. *YouTube*. Google, 19 Jan. 2011. Web. <http://www.youtube.com/watch?v=I4X6cUOQv6w>.

[lxxii] *Dana White,* TMZ.

[lxxiii] Wetzel, "About-Face".

lxxiv Wetzel, "About-Face".

lxxv Wetzel, "About-Face".

lxxvi Erickson, Matt. "Ronda Rousey Meets Liz Carmouche in First UFC Women's Title Fight at UFC 157." *Ronda Rousey Meets Liz Carmouche in First UFC Women's Title Fight at UFC 157*. MMA Junkie, 6 Dec. 2012. Web. 31 May 2013. <http://www.mmajunkie.com/news/2012/12/ronda-rousey-meets-liz-carmouche-in-first-ufc-womens-title-fight-at-ufc-157>.

lxxvii Zuffa, "UFC Primetime."

lxxviii Zuffa, "UFC Primetime."

lxxix Zuffa, "UFC Primetime."

lxxx Zuffa, "UFC Primetime."

lxxxi 'Rowdy Ronda' Rousey Uses Elbow-breaking Signature Move to Win Historic Women's Ultimate Fighting Championships Debut." *Mail Online*. Daily Mail Reporter, 2013. Web. 31 May 2013. <http://www.dailymail.co.uk/news/article-2284250/Ronda-Rousey-fight-Rowdy-Ronda-uses-elbow-breaking-signature-wins-historic-womens-Ultimate-Fighting-Championships-debut.html>.

lxxxii Cruz, Jason. "UFC 157: Payout Perspective." *MMAPayout.com*. N.p., 25 Feb. 2013. Web. 31 May 2013. <http://mmapayout.com/2013/02/ufc-157-payout-perspective/>.

lxxxiii *Good Day LA*. KTTV. Los Angeles, California, 8 Mar. 2013. Television.

lxxxiv *Good Day LA*

lxxxv *Bold Predictions for UFC Star Ronda Rousey's Future*. By Jonathan Snowden. *Bleacher Report*. Turner Broadcasting System, 7 Mar. 2013. Web. 31 May 2013. <http://bleacherreport.com/articles/1558339-bold-predictions-for-ufc-star-ronda-rouseys-future>.

lxxxvi Thomas, Luke. "Technique Talk: Dave Camarillo on Judo in MMA and the Challenge of Ronda Rousey." *MMA*

Fighting. SB Nation, 2013. Web. 02 June 2013.
<http://www.mmafighting.com/2013/6/1/4385780/technique-talk-dave-camarillo-judo-mma-ronda-rousey-blueprint-mma-news>.

[lxxxvii] Krutzik, Ramona, Dr. "Dr. Ramona Krutzik, M.D. Discusses Possible Advantages Fallon Fox May Have." Interview by Steph Daniels. *Bloody Elbow*. SB Nation, 20 Mar. 2013. Web. 31 May 2013.
<http://www.bloodyelbow.com/2013/3/20/4128658/dr-ramona-krutzik-endocrinologist-discusses-possible-advantages-fallon-fox-has>.

[lxxxviii] Raimondi, Marc. "UFC Women's Champ Rousey Weighs in on Transgender Fighter Controversy." *New York Post*. NYP Holdings, 10 Apr. 2013. Web. 31 May 2013.
<http://www.nypost.com/p/blogs/the_main_event/ufc_women_champ_weighs_in_on_transgender_3x7mCaaXn27HVq1Qtu O5lN#axzz2UuYrdpuI>.

Made in the USA
Lexington, KY
31 October 2014